To The
SUPERNATURAL

RUTH LEE

authorHOUSE'

AuthorHouse™
1663 Liberty Drive
Bloomington, IN 47403
www.authorhouse.com
Phone: 833-262-8899

Published by AuthorHouse 09/25/2020

ISBN: 978-1-6655-0111-8 (sc)
ISBN: 978-1-6655-0110-1 (e)

Print information available on the last page.

CONTENTS

PREFACE

There are many paths in a Christian's life. There are paths of prayer, paths of dedication, and paths that lead to tests and trials. Many of the paths that we must travel are dark, slippery and full of disappointment. Yet, you will see from the experiences that I share with you that each path can lead to a level of growth and victory.

When we are in treacherous places, we must learn to hold firm to that rock which is Christ. We must learn to depend on Him and trust Him when there is seemingly no answer, as we wonder who God is and where He is.

We must ask ourselves the question, *"How well do we know God?"* It is a question that no one can adequately answer, because we don't know, and cannot imagine how great God is. We know from the Bible that God is beyond comprehension or understanding. Paul said, *"That I may know Him, and the power of His resurrection and in the fellowship of His sufferings being made conformable to His death"* (Phil. 3:10 KJV). This indicates that "knowing God" is possible.

As I search for God and go to heights and depths that are beyond my intellectual capacity, my spirit seems to demand more. I have to wonder how far I can go. Is there a point of attaining all that God has for me? The answer is most likely no. We will never know Him as He is in this lifetime.

There are questions in the pursuit of "knowing God". Who on earth has found out all there is to know about God? What do others know about him that I don't know? Can we all understand Him on the same level? How deep is that knowledge alone? Often our heart longs to go where He is in His Glory so we can understand Him to the fullest. Ephesians 2:7 NKJV says: *"That in the ages to come he might show the exceeding riches of his grace in his kindness toward us through Christ Jesus."*

As you read, may you be encouraged to begin a new prayer life that will be more than a habit or a necessity when there are problems in your life. May you allow God to call you to a similar experience of growing in Him and knowing Him, in ways you have never experienced before *as He did for me.*

Certain situations challenged me to rise at least two hours before time to go to work and sit in a dark quiet place. There, I began to call on Him to purify my life, cleanse my mind, and to teach me how to be real with Him. In a closer walk, He may require you to reveal all of your secret failures to Him.

As you do this, you will develop a more intimate relationship with Him that will start you on a road to a greater victory than ever before. He may reveal to you that no matter where you are now, *there is always more in God.*

As I share the many ways in which God has worked in people's lives to train, develop character and to purify the mind; I trust that you will find Him in a new and comforting way that generates new growth in your relationship with Him. During this time, may He show you victory, healing, and success as He did for my life and the people who have allowed me to share in their lives.

INTRODUCTION

As you read my life story of prayers and miracles in the last few chapters of this book, you will be experiencing extraordinary visions and supernatural visitations. The knowledge I have gained through the past 55 years from pastors, prophecy teachers, intense study, and what God spoke to me during a recent illness, which I have woven together for this book and is based on what I experienced.

I was in the hospital for several weeks, followed by rehab centers for several months. Throughout my stay there, many things happened to help me understand God's plan much better. God began speaking to me about Creation, from "eternity past through eternity future".

His encounters took place while I was going through surgery. I was asleep, but my spirit is alert. I had several encounters with God. I experienced His Presence and talked with Him.

I also experienced the black darkness of Satan's kingdom as he made a horrendous attack on my faith from this. These encounters seemed to happen when my heart had stopped and it did many times, before they put the pacemaker in.

I want to help those who are interested, to understand that it is extremely important that we are aware of the enemy who will do anything to destroy you and your faith. Nothing is easy when you are working for God. We have an enemy to fight all along the way.

A good scripture to put into practice during your walk with God is, Nehemiah 4:17 KJV, which says to do your work with one hand while having a sword in the other hand. I pray that you will learn many truths from this presentation.

CHAPTER 1

❧

The Beginning

As the story of my life of many miracles unfolds, my prayer is those of you who are fhhacing difficult situations in your life, family, or church will be able to glean from my experiences.

In Bellville, Pennsylvania in 1897 there was a young man by the name of Rufus Zook Byler born to Abiah J. and Lydia Byler. My dad, R.Z. Byler, was raised in a Mennonite Home and community.

Far removed from us today, this primitive way of life featured plain clothes, horse-drawn buggies, wood stoves, washboards, and wells along with strict moral standards of that era. Some years before, my dad's mother, Lydia Zook

Byler, died on Christmas day as she was departing this life to take up a new residence with Jesus, she said, *"Look!"* pointing toward the window. *"There is Jesus and my baby."* The baby had died very young.

After her death, his dad married again and things were not the same. it seems the step mom was a task master and even though my papa was a very hard steady worker it was really hard for him. As he was always a very spirited and zealous man might have had some baring in it.

While working in his family's wheat field as a young teenager in Pennsylvania, the Lord called my dad to repentance. He knelt at a stump in the middle of the field and gave his heart to the Lord.

When my papa was a young man, he heard about the Pentecostal movement which was relatively new to the United States. This movement had manifested in a group of people in a storefront on Azusa Street in California in the early 1900's. These people had come together to pray and during this time; the Holy Spirit began to manifest Himself to them. Some people were given sermons, others given healings, and some would express emotions given by the Holy Spirit.

Over time, a denomination was formed and in 1914, a group of ministers came together to form what we now know as the Assemblies of God. Ever since that time, missions have been a huge part of this fellowship. Now, around the world, the Assemblies of God has grown to 67,000,000 members. This is what the power of the Holy Spirit can do through people who surrender all to God.

One day while working in the fields with his brother Levi, a thunderstorm rolled in. They stood under a large tree for shelter and Levi was struck by lightning and instantly killed.

After his brother's death, my papa, as we called him, more fervently sought God and began his pursuit in the Pentecostal movement. As Papa was searching for a deeper experience with God, he read of Jesus praying in the mountains.

He went up on a mountain in his area and had an encounter that was different than anything he had experienced before. He came down from the mountain after a few days and told his pastor and his daddy about his encounter with God. However, they were not ready to believe what he was telling them about his experience.

Shortly after, in 1918, when he was approximately 20 years old, he heard about the Assemblies of God. He began his pursuit of the new church denomination and ended up at the headquarters in Arkansas.

There, he met Woodworth Etta, a great revivalist at that time. He asked her how to receive the baptism of the Holy Spirit. She instructed him to go to an upstairs room and to stay there until he received the baptism. Three days later and fasting during that time, he returned from that room full of the Holy Spirit and fire.

After that, Woodworth Etta paired him with another young evangelist. They were sent to Tuscaloosa, Alabama and from there to Clanton, Alabama.

During their time of ministry in Alabama, many people were saved and filled with the baptism in the Holy Spirit. He helped build many churches across Alabama, Mississippi, and Florida. My mother learned about Christ through his ministry and after her conversion, they fell in love and were married. God later blessed them with four children.

About 1919, when my dad launched out and held his first revival in Alabama, the first place my dad preached after coming to Clanton, Alabama was in old Macedonia Baptist church. However, they soon asked him to leave because they did not believe in the Baptism of the Holy Spirit. With his new converts he built his first church and named it New Hope, organized it in the Assemblies of God, and soon went on to two other areas nearby and established churches.

He did all of this with very little money but the people had a mind to work. The only support he and mom had come from the church. It was in the form of an occasional chicken or if someone killed a hog we might get a piece of meat, but never money. dad always had a garden and raised animals for meat. Even in times of need, we helped others. We were a very giving family and I believe that is the reason why we were never without the necessities of life.

My mother's sister Lue Smith opened her home and they began what was called a protracted meeting. After they got enough members she suggested we build a church. Lue would provide the land and timber and a man in the congregation offered timber also. The community came together and built the church. Dad would oversee the work since he had carpentry skills.

Because the people were united they agreed to call the church New Harmony. At the end of my parents' lives they were both buried there in the church yard on a strip of land given to him for that purpose by the man he purchased the land from. I think of the place we lived as the old home place because we lived here longer than in other areas. I can remember more because I was a little older now. Recently the community built a new church on the property where our former house was located.

May 1927: Our family moved to Lewistown, Pennsylvania where my dad was from. Many other Byler's had settled in the Mennonite village. I believe the area was named after the Byler's which was originally spelled Bieler.

Just before I was born, my dad had appendicitis and in the 1929 era, medical science was not advanced as it is now.

Before he received medical treatment the doctor said he had developed an infection called gangrene, which was found in hernias and other areas of the body. Because of the lack of proper medical treatment, he eventually died.

When the doctor told my mother she began to call on God. She explained to Him how she was not capable of taking care of three small children and supporting them especially in the middle of the great depression in 1929 where there were few jobs and no government support of any type.

Since she was in Pennsylvania and her family in Alabama made it a difficult situation. She told God how she needed him. She stood over the bed where his body was laying and called desperately upon God, just as God said in His Word, if you will call on me in time of trouble I will hear you and show you great and mighty things. My dad instantly came to life and got out of bed totally healed with no more medical problems.

My dad was a man of his word and in his exalted emotions he told God he would always trust him with his physical body. Until it was his time to leave this world and be with the Lord, he kept that promise.

I don't remember my dad ever being in the bed sick or even complaining about feeling bad after that. He was always working when bad things happened to him. He would sing, *I Feel Like Traveling On*. It seemed he found a depth of faith I would like to know. If my mother had not called my daddy back to life, I would not be here today because it was about a year or two after that when I was born.

It was on March 8, 1930 in Lewistown, Pennsylvania when I was born into this great God fearing family. My brothers and sister watched the doctor when he arrived at our house with his little black bag. It was a normal thing in those days for the doctor to make house calls. My brothers and sister were watching from an upstairs bedroom as the doctor came down the walkway with his little black bag and shortly after he arrived they heard a baby cry. They thought he had brought me to mama in that little black bag. Of course that was before little children knew about how babies got here. It seems we've gone to the extreme in the other direction because sex to a child now seems almost normal to discuss even outside of marriage.

It was not easy in those days for my dad being Dutch, Mennonite, and now a Pentecostal preacher. Those were three strikes against him but he never wavered and was very zealous for God and His work. He was no longer accepted in the Mennonite church or by his family. It was not long, about May 1930 until our family moved back to Alabama.

When we moved back, my family resumed their work in the church and the Assemblies of God movement was still full of life. This life was coming from a result of the fresh outpouring of God's Spirit in the early 1900's at Azusa Street in California.

In 1932, after moving back to Alabama, we lived on a dairy farm where my dad would work to help support the ministry and his family. In the early 1930's the church did not support the pastor especially in a new work like he was a part of, so he had to work a full time job and minister as well.

While we were there, an airport was built about a mile from our house. Airplanes were always fascinating to me. I had a special interest in them because they would have small air shows that intrigued me, except for the frightening acts such as spiraling downward. I thought as they would go out of my sight behind the trees that the plane crashed, and that put a fear of flying in me that has been hard to overcome. We moved from there in 1936.

Every child needs someone close to be strong and loving in order to mature in a normal way. My parents were loving people, a wonderful family, hard working, and always kept a close relationship with one another. We always had time for relatives and friends as they would come unannounced to visit. Those were times when people preferred one another.

We also had many evangelists visit and stay at our home if they had come to conduct a revival. Some even moved in with us as they would itinerate between mission assignments. One who stayed with us was Reverend Smith.

They had just arrived from South America and in a short time all of us children contracted malaria.

It seems as though they brought some mosquitoes or larvae in their luggage and they got into our well and made us all so sick. It seems I had a more difficult time than the other siblings. I was somewhere between four and six years old but I made the best of it. The only cure known at that time for malaria was quinine, and I detested taking it. Reverend Smith offered to buy me a red tam (a small round cap) that I really liked if I would take my medication. That worked for me because I had wanted one for a long time.

My sister, Louise and I were far apart in age but for several years we were play mates. When she was about ten we built a play house, pretending to cook and care for our children. I learned a lot from her but it wasn't long until she was no longer interested in playing, so I moved on with her to more mature ways of entertaining ourselves. I suppose it was her guidance that caused me to mature at a younger age than normal. After all I had to keep up with her because our community was sparsely populated and there was no one else to play with. There is an advantage to being the youngest child. I learned from all of the family some good things and some not so well.

The best way I know to explain my life is to say what a wonderful family I had. We were taught to always be polite to anyone who might come to visit no matter how inconvenient it might be at the time, whether it was relatives or friends as they would come many times unannounced to visit.

My mother kept an eye on me because of my determination to do some things she did not allow. My best friend lived about a block from my house and mama did not give me permission to visit her. After all, I was five years old now and thought I should be able to do a few things without asking mama. I went to my friend's house but soon I heard my mom calling me and fear came over me because she believed that to spare the rod would spoil the child. I learned that day to get permission before I visited my friend.

While living at the Dairy farm where my dad was working, our house had a large barn with a high peak. My brother, David and I were on the roof playing and he got my parents' large black umbrella and said it would work like a parachute. I had watched guys jump out of those airplanes and he told me I should jump. It turned inside out and swoosh I hit the ground. David threatened me if I told my mother so I kept it to myself.

It was a year or two later in 1937 when we moved to another city where God was calling my dad to start another church. That was my first memory of a bush arbor meeting. While dad was forming a congregation to begin a church he would use the bush arbor, and eventually used a tent.

In the bush arbors they used two nail kegs at each end of a board for pews. During those services the fire of God was burning in the hearts of people. There were lots of shouting and dancing in the Spirit. That is when I learned that it is not the type of singing, music, or even preaching that God is impressed with, or that will draw a crowd but it is the sincere heart and the fire of God that will draw people. They will come even without air conditioners, carpets or fancy décor.

Prior to beginning school, my brother Paul broke his leg while he was playing baseball and was home for several weeks. He and I got involved in picking up nails around a barn our dad had built and made it a project to straighten the nails to be used again. I was a preschooler so he began to teach me how to count, then how to add, and then how to multiply. He taught me all the multiplication tables and ABC's. He also taught me how to tell time and how to print and then to write.

I was to start school the next year and I was ready. It was an unforgettable day. My first day at school, the teacher asked if anyone could print their name. I said I could. Then she asked if anyone could tell time. She asked questions until she found out about all the things I could do and she was very amazed. She took me by the hand and led me to all the junior high and high school classrooms to show them what I could do, and have me tell what I knew.

I found out that my dad had taught Paul all of those things and the same thing happened to him at his school about six years earlier. I suppose he was just passing it on.

It was at the age of eight that I realize I had missed out on so much as a child. Life seemed normal to me. I was old enough now to understand when my family talked about the great depression in 1929. When I was born in 1930 I had no tricycle, dolls or other toys. My mom had to make me rag dolls because there was only enough money to buy the necessities.

My brother David was a little jealous of the fact that I got his blanket he loved so much, but we were in the heart of the depression years and could not buy a new blanket. It is quite difficult to explain that to a three year old. David mentioned that blanket even after he had children of his own.

Our family was a very light hearted and joyful family. Even when David seemed to enjoy telling me what I had missed when I was small and told me about their toys, siblings just do that to each other at times, I was happy with my life because you don't miss things you never had. Happiness and contentment is what counts and I thought we had everything we needed.

1938: From that city we moved near an area called Pools Cross Road where we started protracted meetings to form another congregation and build another church. My dad was the pastor there for several years. This is the location where he originally started when he came to Alabama.

It was during these years that God began to draw me to Himself. I tried to give my life to him so I asked one of the evangelists, Reverend Cook, how to be saved. He told me to believe on the Lord and I would be saved but in my youthful mind I thought he was saying that sometime during my life I would be saved. That stayed with me and helped me when I finally did give my heart to the Lord. This was our life style for all of my formative years. We were a family who was taught the Word of God and Christian principals, and how to love people and God.

As my parents grew older, my mother became very ill with a brain tumor that had bothered her for many years. Doctors didn't know what was wrong with her because medical science had not yet developed a method of testing for that disease. My dad stayed home more and used his carpentry skills and opened a tent making shop. He made tents as long as he lived and continued building churches and preaching the gospel.

We were all musically inclined although not professionally trained. We all had an ear for music and played an instrument and sang. We would sit on the front porch, playing and singing. Mom played the organ which was just inside the door. David played the steel guitar. Paul was very good on the guitar. Louise and I would play the mandolin. Daddy did not play an instrument, but he was a good singer. Our Dad and mother were very good singers. My brother Paul has a cassette tape of them singing and when I heard it I was pleasantly surprised.

Later, my brother David developed his talent and joined Reeb and Rabe's band that played on the radio in Birmingham, Alabama. He played the steel guitar for the group and would occasionally sing. Later, he appeared on the Grand Ole Opry and then went on to teach music in a Bible school in Dallas, Texas. Both of my brothers and their children were always involved in music in the church.

My dad was not a farmer as we know them here in Alabama. In Pennsylvania wheat farms was the main crop so planting cotton and corn was not his specialty. My mom, being raised on a farm, was a big help to him. For over the next few years we worked hard taking care of the two cows and two mules, lots of chickens, pigs and a huge garden. One thing that makes me feel very special is my family. Perhaps we had not always been the highest on the social ladder, but I believe the happiness we shared surpassed that of most families and was far more valuable to me than our social status.

When I received a copy of the *Byler Family Tree* I realized how blessed by God we are, and what an awesome thing to have such a wonderful heritage. Oh, they were nowhere near perfect or not always theologically correct on some issues, but for hundreds of years, men and women served and worked for God in many capacities, such as bishops, deacons and church leaders. Having originated from the Mennonite religion, we were not the most popular people but there was lots of love.

1940: We received letters from our family circle once a month which caused me to never question whether or not any of my aunts and uncles were anything but God fearing people. Their letters would begin something like this, *"Greetings in the lovely name of our Lord and Savior Jesus Christ,"* followed by many other words of praise and glory to God. It seemed to me their lives were totally given to God. It could be they were attempting to convert my dad since he was now Pentecostal, which they thought at that time, was a false religion.

Being a Pentecostal family made it difficult to develop relationships because at that time there were very few holiness people, and we were considered a cult. I managed to find a few peers and we quickly became friends.

We all had chores and mine was to get the eggs out of the nest. I got pecked in the eye once, and I also helped with feeding the animals. I always liked to milk the cows, and of course I had made close friends with all of the animals except the pigs. The animals would follow me around. My parents' good planning caused us to have plenty of meat and vegetables year round. We would can meat, soup, all kind of vegetables and fruits, cured pork in the smoke house and many other clever ideas they had, made it such fun and a great deal of togetherness.

I had one pet that I wanted to keep in the house but mama was too clean for an animal to be in the house, and thought the little bantam hen would make a mess. However, I had pretty much house trained her and I would take the small oval braided rug and make her a nest. She would not move until I told her to as she was either well trained or she was afraid of mom's broom. She lived to be twelve years old. I kept her six years and then we were moving again so I gave her to a cousin and he kept her six more years.

We were a Pentecostal family and my Dad was from the north and there were very few Pentecostal people in that area, so we were considered unusual. I managed to find a few peers and we became friends. One girl asked me to go with her outside to play during recess one day, but she had other things in mind. It seemed she had a stepfather and things were not going well at their house so we sat down in the school yard and she took a piece of glass and a rock and began to break the glass into tiny pieces. I did not know what her intentions were so I just watched as she told me a little about her home life, gathered up the shivers of glass put them in her mouth and swallowed them, and then tried to get me to promise not to tell. I could not do that so I ran and told the teacher and that is the last time I remember seeing her. However, I heard that she did not die.

1942: Paul was the oldest child and when the war started in 1942, he was called into the army. This was very disturbing to all of us especially my mother. It seems she cried most of the time while he was gone especially while he was overseas in the war zone. He was an ambulance driver and he had to go to the front lines to pick up wounded soldiers. God kept him safe and I believe it was by prayer and faith that kept him through the war.

Since my dad was an evangelist and a church planter, we moved quite frequently which made it hard for the children to adjust. In those days we dressed differently and long hair was a must. Long sleeves on our long dresses, and absolutely no pants were a part of our dress code. Who says that can't be altered a little, to keep my peers from being cruel to me? Since my mother made most of our clothes I would have her make my skirts and blouses so I could roll the skirt up to a modern length which was just below the knee, and push my sleeves up. And, there you go, I was somewhat in style. It was not that I wanted to be rebellious. I just didn't like people to laugh at me.

1943 We moved to another area and I was in a new school. I was a little older now and started to fix my hair more stylish. That year I noticed one of the boys noticing me. In those days there were no lunch rooms so we would take our lunch to school and one day, Russell asked me if I would eat lunch with him. We went around to the side of the school and sat on the steps and had a good time just talking and laughing as we ate. When we moved away from there I lost contact with him because there were very few phones at that time.

It was about eight years later when I saw him and he was married by then though there was still a place in my heart for him. Not love or a crush or anything such as that, just pleasant thoughts from the past. I suppose he was not judgmental of me even though I was from a Christian home. To me that gave me a sense of belonging and for that I will always have pleasant memories of his kindness.

The First Vision: When I was about 13 years old we moved again, this time to a small farm. Months later my dad rode to town in a wagon to buy a mule. My mama was a very caring and emotional person and began to worry when my dad did not come home and it was getting dark. She realized he could not see very well and she became more bothered as time passed.

Surely God was aware of her concern and came to her rescue so I believe he used me to do that. I told her to not worry that I knew right where he was and for about an hour I told her right where he was. I did not understand why I could see him but I told her every turn he made and when he got in sight of the house I told her to go to the window and look because he was coming around the next corner. She did look and was so astonished that he was right where I told her he was. It just seemed normal to me.

Who knows what a child can get involved. Our community at that time was sparsely populated. The house nearest to us is where Mr. Johnston lived. They had a girl and even though she was much older than I, she and I became friends. We talked a lot and one day she asked me to come and help her squeeze the grapes for her Papa to make juice. I learned that what he was doing was making wine, so we got in a vat full of grapes. I can't remember if I helped pick them or not but with our bare feet we walked and jumped until we had a vat of juice. Yuck, that is disgusting. I don't know who drank the juice but it was not me for sure. My mom was a really clean person who taught us children to be clean so I would not have thought of drinking that juice.

1944: By now we have moved again to Clanton. I didn't care for country living and neither did my sister Louise so we decided on an alternative. She thought she would like to have at least a part time job. She was six years older than I but she never seemed to think I was too young for her to share her ideas with me. I had always kept up with her since she looked younger than I. She was shorter than I, petite and blond and at that time there was no need for proof of age. I applied along with her for jobs and we both found what we were looking for. I always took the lead because she was less aggressive than I, so I would say Louise is twenty and I am eighteen and there was never a question about my age.

That was in the days when people were honest and your word was as good as a notarized paper is now. I suppose it was people like me that caused that to change. I was not a Christian at that time so to me it was a little white lie. (There is no such thing.). We both went to work and my parents never knew what I had done. I convinced them that I needed to work and they did give their consent because it was during the war and our funds were low and businesses were desperate for help.

My boss lived next door to us and he had a daughter the same age as me. He came by my job one day and asked me: *"How old did you say you were?"* I said, *"18"*, and he said, *"Well that is strange. My daughter was born the same time you were and she is only 15."* The Bible says, be sure your sins will find you out. To my surprise he never mentioned it again.

In the long run, this did work out for the best. When we didn't have a farm dad would work as a carpenter. My sister and I thought it was best to pay most of the bills so my dad could evangelize.

Louise and I purchased a 1939 Plymouth with my dad's help of course, and where we lived there was a very large yard. I began to drive backward and forward until I learned to drive. It so happened that our next door neighbor, Miss July, found out that I had been learning to drive. She asked me to take her shopping. I suppose you can tell by now I do not have a lot of fear or apprehension.

Her son was in the military and he had left his little club coupe with her (It had a rumble seat and that was a big thing! in those days). She wanted someone to drive it so I took her shopping. Then one day I went to the court house and applied for my driver's license and got it. I was about fifteen years old but I looked eighteen. As I will explain later, I finally repented for those lies and was forgiven and I highly recommend that people do not do those things because sin always has consequences.

1946: Too much freedom. My dad was a carpenter so he built a house for us. Louise and I paid for the materials. At that point my dad was free to go evangelize and mama would have someone with her. She had become ill and was not able to travel with him anymore. That arrangement worked well; however as it was easy to convince my mom of many things.

At that time it was totally unheard of for a woman to wear pants, but since I was a strong willed person I helped her to see that on my job I had to lean over a lot and that I needed to wear jeans. Shopping was a huge thing with me. I always wore the latest styles and drove a good car. I had many friends and was a very good person. I was in church every time they had a service and I gave money to build a church around the corner from our house. I would sing in the choir and in special groups (never a solo). Then one day I finally gave my heart to the Lord.

I had lived like a Christian all of my life. When I made my commitment decision, the devil really came after me. I did not know at that time anything about his attractions, so he got the advantage over me. The church I was attending had a bad split and I became disillusioned with church. That is when, at the age of eighteen, I quit my job and moved to Birmingham with my cousin and two other women who were living a very loose life.

My first convert (back to 1963-64):

Sometimes God has to get us out of our comfort zone, so He can either use us there, or use the situation to make us stronger. That is what happened on a job that I took as a young Christian in a textile mill. The work was hard and very hot. Soon one of the employees began to help me when I was falling behind on my job. I was a spare-hand which meant that I would work in areas where either the main worker was absent or complete a job that no one wanted to do.

Many times the workers would stay out of work when the job was going to be very hard. The employee who helped me was living in sin at the time. God gave me favor with her and she gladly listened to me but I didn't think she would accept Jesus, but God gave me wisdom to reach out to her. She was very responsive and soon she accepted the Lord and turned out to be a wonderful Christian and friend.

She was such a blessing to me. We prayed together on our breaks, and the Lord was so wonderfully present. She would also come to my house to pray. During one of those times as we prayed God's Presence came into that room. He was so strong that we could not move a muscle or speak for quite some time. God blessed me with the opportunity to help lead her family and relatives to God.

Her dad was quite elderly. One day, Jeannie and I stopped by to visit her parents. She said her dad needed to be saved as he was not well. We got inside and sat down and at that point I seemed to be so abrupt and to the point so I said to him, *"Mr. Woodruff, would you like to be saved?"* To my surprise he said, *"Yes I would."* We prayed with him and I believe I will see him in Heaven one day. God was so gracious to save all of her family, and meet many of their financial needs. They are in another city now, busy in a church there.

It was during this time in my life that I had another experience with God. I was working in another room filling in for the person who ran the job. I was praying when the Holy Spirit manifested Himself in that place in a cloud. The frames of yarn where I worked were open enough so that you could see the person on the other side. At that time, it was an elderly man who I did not know very well.

When God took me into the Glory Cloud, all I could see was as a thick smoke so his face that was visible but not clear. I could see his eyes and they were steadfast on me and I wondered later what he saw that evening as God spoke to me about my family's salvation. I had the permission in that moment to ask for as many family members as I wanted to be saved, so I began to name them and I know that when I get to Heaven I will see everyone of them.

My brothers and sisters were so wonderful, especially Paul. After the war, he returned home, started his family and built a house with daddy's help. He was the oldest of the four and his life was an example of spiritual uprightness. I always thought of him as a God fearing man with lots of wisdom. He was so good to everyone including me. If I was going to pattern my life after any one it would be him. He was a Sunday school teacher, Deacon and a great family man with four children all serving the Lord. He married Mary Walker and they had four wonderful children Annette, Lois, Jerry and Sharon.

I loved and respected Louise because she was so smart. As a teen she could do all the things I wanted to do, but I suppose that was a normal thing since she was six years older than I was and a head taller. However I tried to keep up with her and would try to take the lead in some areas.

As a teen I was far more adventurous than she was in many things, however she would try to hold me back enough so I would not get in trouble with my parents. Had it not been for her we would not have kept our curfew very often. I suppose you could say I would rather suffer the consequences than to keep the rules. She married and had three fine children, Diane, Kay, and Ronnie. There seemed to be lots of love in their home.

David was the red head. I was close to him in my young days, but we did not see eye to eye on very many things as siblings. He was older and I would do a lot of things he said because I thought he knew more than I did. However, most of the time, it would get me into bad situations. David became a minister and teacher. He married Vesta Aaron in the 1940's and they had two girls, Martha and Faye. They moved to another state but later when the girls were in their teens I was in great sorrow when Vesta and the girls moved out West. Life has many changes that are not always pleasant, Vesta was very kind to me, and I will always love her.

In later years, David married Charlotte and they had five children, Karen, Darlene, Cathy, Connie, and Johnny. All seven of David's children are healthy and good looking.

There was so much love in my mother's family that I hardly knew who was the blood relative or the in law, because I loved their spouses and they seemed to love me the same. I trust that I will see every one of my relatives in Heaven on that day.

To me, my mother was the greatest mom ever. She had such a strong love that was very giving. She never seemed to think of herself before others. She was an excellent pastor's wife and mother. She suffered many headaches, nausea, pain and sickness due to the brain tumor she had. It was called acromegaly which causes the bones to grow and that caused pressure on nerves and cells causing other complications.

Those complications resulted in four major surgeries over the years and at that point no doctor seemed to be able to find the cause for her headaches, stomach problems and all the other things she suffered. Despite her illness it never affected her relationships or attention that she gave to her family. She was always there when we were sick or hurt. She was the best. Because of the love of God in our family I barely noticed the lack of THINGS and at that time I thought we had everything.

I attribute my next actions to being naïve about the ways of the nonbeliever. I had been raised in a Christian environment. Going to work on my first job, I fell prey to the devil's devices not knowing anything about how people lived who were not Christians. As for the schools, they were not as they are today. We began classes with prayer and Bible reading, and the teachers were aware of what took place with their students. There was punishment for doing wrong, so I was of the opinion that everybody was good and moral.

Because of my state of mind, I *allowed* conflict in my soul when I began to work around people who were not limited to clean living. Being influenced by the world, I was a target for the devil. About that time in my life the church that I told you about earlier where I attended split, and I was disillusioned by some things that I heard which turned to hatred for all Christians.

When I moved to another city, Satan was waiting for me in the form of a housewife who allowed me to move in with her so I could help with her children while she dated a married man. Her husband worked out of town, so she was free to live that lifestyle. A strange thing happened as I took my first steps into the unknown world of sin. I was sitting in a large night club with a group and my inexperienced mind thought, *"I sure am glad I am not like these people"* however, I was sitting in the same place they were. I was doing the same things they were doing but my heart had not fully turned away from God at that point.

For the next year I ran from God and even turned on the church and then the dreams began. The night was a night of horror, but because I always had a high respect for God it started me in another direction. I was sleeping in the room with two very wicked women. I was the children's nana, and although I had no respect for those women, I really cared for the children.

That night, I dreamed the place where I was became surrounded with fire. There were billows of flames surrounding me as far as I could see. Only a narrow path was open and the Lord spoke to me in no uncertain terms. He said, *"You can leave through the opening, or be eternally lost. This is the only time you have, and the only path out for you. I hurried out the path."*

I woke up startled, and I went into the kitchen, sat down and pondered what I had just experienced. I made up my mind to turn from that way of life the best way I knew how. I did everything within my own ability because at the time I did not know about God's ability. I did not repent at that point. However, that started me on a right course. I moved back to my home town, away from those people who were influencing me in a bad way. When I moved back home I tried to change, but self-righteousness is not what God desires for us.

1953: Almost certain death. I did escape my former life and I started a ten-year journey back to God. That journey was not without many unexplainable things. Several times I found myself facing devastating situations, one of them being a night about two years later. Something happened which I believe was a time when God was trying to get my attention, or either trying to scare the devil out of me.

The story goes like this. At that time during the 1950s, it was a relatively drug free society. People were more trustworthy than in the time we live in now, and I was not as alert to the tricks of the devil as I should have been. Being away from God is called being in darkness and there is danger in the darkness. I was facing almost certain death that night. I had once known the right way and had departed from it.

I was working at a business where my bosses were also my friends and they brought a young man in one day. He was very nice looking and well-mannered as were my boss and his wife. After a few visits, he asked me if he could take me home from work. I thought he was not acting like himself, but I said sure. That turned out to be one of the most frightening nights of my life. Instead of going toward my house, he turned the opposite direction, and when I asked why, he said, *"You will see."*

I realized that he was really acting strangely, so as he was turning off of the main road I opened the door and jumped out into a large ditch. It had to be the grace of God that I was not severely injured. By the time I landed in the ditch he was standing over me saying I could have killed you before you hit the ground and he forced me back into the car. He began to put on gloves and pulled a gun out from under the seat.

I began to plead for my life which it seemed he did

not even hear. He kept saying, *"You will never do this to me again."* I would ask him what he was talking about but there was no response, and he would say something like you will not do that to me again. At that time, I realized that I was going to die and I knew I would not go to Heaven. There is only one place left, and I made up my mind that if other people could make it in hell I could too. That is the very most imprudent thing I ever thought in my life.

I tried again to talk about other things, but he kept holding the gun. I tried over and over to talk to him and eventually he began to go in and out of his stupor. I started to get through to him a little, enough to talk him into going to a certain place to get something to eat, play some music and try to work things out. I knew by now that he thought I was someone else, so he turned around and headed back toward my house.

He began to tell me that he had taken too much morphine and he told me who he thought I was. I said, *"I have been working all day and I need to change clothes to go to the restaurant we talked about."* In his present state of mind, I suppose he did not think about the fact that I just might not come back, but I believe that was also God.

I went into my apartment to get dressed, but I did not go back out. I was so frightened and for days I was afraid because he told me if I reported him, he would come back and kill me. I called the police but they said they couldn't do anything unless he had committed some act of violence. I think he was a friend of the police. He worked at Capitol Chevrolet and he knew so many people and was a well-respected young man.

CHAPTER 2

❊

My Family Life

Family life always seemed good to me with all of the activity of us children, chores, and family meals. We looked forward to bedtime Bible stories and to the next day. When I became engaged to Hubert I had something special to look forward to where I could experience my own home. Safety of home was always comforting to me especially having gone through the experience of the year before. After all, I had some quite devastating experiences while I was so young, growing up too fast and suffering many setbacks during my teen years. I was the object of very undeserving criticism. I needed the safety of home.

I was not comfortable with the dating scene and many

unsure relationships so when I met Hubert Lee, a wonderful story began to unfold. Vesta brought me to Montgomery, Alabama and helped me find a job. I was working at Tony's drive in restaurant as a car hop as they were called back then. Hubert was a customer there. He came every night, got a cup of coffee and would leave with just a thank you and a good night.

But something was happening that I did not comprehend at the time. A little later, I went inside and told Mrs. Argus who was the owner's wife, there was a man outside that I am going to marry. I did not even know his name. That was in December and a few weeks later he started talking to me. He asked me if he could take me home and he did. It was not anything special, just a ride home.

The next week, he told me he was going to North Carolina to visit his mother. He also told me he was in the Air Force and would be on furlough until January. When he returned he came back again for his coffee so we would talk. Then he asked to take me home again. This time we talked a little more and he told me about some of his life experiences. He started to show interest in me as someone he liked very much and he took me home for the rest of January.

We talked and talked until I felt I got to know him very well. One of the attractions I had for him was he was trusting and encouraging. Not only that but he was polite and respectful of me and he treated me like a lady. One night we were talking and he asked me if I would like to have a check every month. Then he said he would like to have his own home. Some of you might have taken that the wrong way but you can't draw a dependent's check if you are not married. We set the wedding date for February 12.

Only one thing went wrong. None of our pictures developed so we have no wedding pictures. However it was a only a justice of the peace ceremony in their home with his wife and my best friend with us. It was a precious occasion with true love, not passion like so many today.

It was during those years that I met Hubert Lee and a wonderful story began to unfold. We were married in about a year we began our family which was two girls. They brought great joy to our lives.

The marriage was wonderful until 1962 when I accepted Jesus as my Savior which I will address in the next chapter. My husband and I lived good moral lives, but we were not Christians. It was years later that we became involved in a more secular lifestyle. After meeting people who liked to party, I was back into my former party life style. We all were very close in relationship and always enjoyed each other's company. I understand that when it comes to spiritual growth, you don't stand still. You either go forward or backward.

1955: Hubert was assigned to Japan, and for the months

before I joined him, I was living temporally with my mother in law who owned a domiciliary. For this reason, I was around a great deal of sickness and dying. To my amazement, as I listened to the screams of an elderly woman who had a short time to live, I became aware that she was going into eternity and perhaps was not saved. I thought about trying to tell her about Jesus, but there were so many people around that I was hesitant.

As I became more concerned about her soul I made up my mind that if everyone would leave I would talk to her (which was not likely since she was so near death), but to my surprise everyone left the room. Most were gone to do some shopping for the needs of the people. I went to her bed and said, *"Lady, I don't know if you know Jesus or not but it is time for you to consider Him"* and I told her the best I knew about how to be saved. She showed signs of being aware of what I was saying. Hopefully she prayed with me in my very crude manner. I will have to leave that to God.

I also ministered to a man who was also dying. I did not know God at that point. It was years later that I became a Christian and I have wondered how I knew how to tell them how to be saved when I did not know how to receive Christ myself. That is one of the wonders of God.

CHAPTER 3

❧

Trip to Japan

1955: Leaving my home and family was not easy. My dad took me to the airport in Montgomery, Alabama on my way to Japan and for the first time in my life, I saw my daddy cry as the plane was taxing down the runway. Little did he know that within just minutes, our lives would be in danger and I was not ready to meet my Maker. I knew he was praying and it could be that is what held the plane together as the pilot flew into a violent storm that was more than the pilot was aware of. In the air we were tossed about like a toy.

One minute I could see the ground and the next minute, the clouds. We had no warning to fasten our seat belts so we went right through the turbulence as I tried to hold on to Laura who was sixteen months old. Debbie was holding onto the seat. It was an undesirable experience I will not likely forget. I welcomed the sight of the Chicago airport so I could get my feet on the ground.

My flight was delayed in Chicago as a result of a problem that occurred during our take off. I was already frightened so badly from the storm we had just come through. I was ready to go home. On arrival at the Washington airport another scene occurred that was devastating to me. At the time, Laura had not yet started walking and Debbie was three years old. When we got off the plane, it was at the far end of the plane terminal and it was about one half mile to the front.

Everyone rushed to where they were going, so I was left alone with a situation. Laura had to be carried along with an overnight bag and one suitcase and I had a three-year-old who was not big enough to help carry anything. For the next thirty minutes or so I would take Laura about fifty yards and leave her with Debbie while I went back to pick up the luggage and take it about fifty yards beyond them. I did that until I reached the front on the terminal.

Both of the girls were good natured. After calling a taxi we went to the base where we would stay for a couple of days while we waited for the departure of our ship to Japan.

Upon departure, I noticed Laura was breaking out on her body. I took her to see the doctor, and they told me to use Ivory soap because she seemed to be allergic to what I was using. I did not believe that but what could I do.

After we boarded the ship, I noticed that the rash was much worse and was covering her body. The ship set sail and we were in a small cabin with another lady and her child, bunk beds and a crib, no walking room, and a small bathroom. The lady, Debbie and I, were all getting motion sickness which we had all the way to Japan. Meanwhile Laura was getting a temperature and I knew by then she needed attention. I took her to the ship doctor and he said that she had the red measles. She was really sick for weeks.

There was a day the ship had a fire drill and everyone had to go on deck. We were headed towards Alaska and there was ice on deck, so I went to the doctor and got permission to stay in the cabin. We arrived in Adak, Alaska in a few days, and we were allowed to leave the ship to shop. By that time, the lady in the cabin with us and I had worked out a plan for going on deck, eating and going off ship. I would keep her child while she moved around and she would do the same for me.

On our way to Japan after we departed from Alaska we were told that a mail ship had broken in half and we had to go back about a day and a half journey to pick up the passengers. By the time we arrived to pick them up, they were almost frozen, but they did survive. In a few days, Debbie started showing signs of measles, so I had two sick children and we would be arriving in Japan in approximately a week.

They were saying that the ship would have to be quarantined when we arrived and no one would be allowed to leave the ship. However, Debbie did not have them as severely as Laura and she and the little boy in the cabin with us improved enough in time for us to leave the ship when we arrived. If I had been a Christian it would have been much easier.

What a surprise we had as we started to our new home. The whole country was so drab. Nothing was painted, and the houses were so different in style. There was no grass in the yards. My opinion of Japan had always been that it was a colorful place, but I suppose it was from seeing all of the things in the past that had made Japan very beautiful.

Then we arrived at Tachikawa where the AFB was located. The stores were all open front, but the city was colorful and nice, totally different from anything I had ever seen. There were hundreds of bicycles and some small cars. You had to almost merge into the maze of bicycles which was the main transportation there at that time.

1956: By now I had joined Hubert on a three year tour of duty in Japan. Even then, the Lord was dealing with my heart about my spiritual life. I waited for a letter from home and at the same time I really dreaded reading my daddy's letters because he always ended his letters with *"Don't wait too long to get right with God."*

It was in those days that God began to draw me to Himself. The Bible says that you cannot be saved unless the Spirit draws you and again God began to communicate with me through dreams and visions. At this point, I would not attend church or listen to any Christians at all. God found a way and that was through the dreams. They were so frightening that I would wake up praying for God to help me to not be lost.

Our home in Japan, which Hubert had ready for us when we arrived, was all furnished with rattan furniture which he bought from a family whose tour of duty had ended (we had stored our furniture back in the USA). The house was not painted and located in the rural area of Tachikawa, Japan where the rice patties were located.

The first thing I noticed was the odor. Rice patties were fertilized with human waste that was put into open pits until it was distributed to the fields. In the spring you would see the workers swiftly working in the rice patties transplanting the rice in watery fields. Our house was located near these fields and they could be seen from our living room window which was a very spectacular sight especially when they were ready to harvest. The rows were so straight and long. The fields were large and it was a sight to behold.

Our home was located in plain view of beautiful snowcapped, Mount Fujiyama which is a well-known volcanic mountain. Just after we arrived in Japan, Laura got sick again and I had to walk about a half mile in the rain (because it was the rainy season at that time) to get a bus to take her to the base doctor. He told me that she had pneumonia.

I also hired a native girl named Kaiko as a maid and baby sitter. That was one of the first good things that happened after arrival. She was so good with the girls and she had Laura speaking the Japanese language before she spoke English. Very near our home, there was a small zoo, and after Kaiko had worked for us over a year, she asked me if she could take Debbie to the zoo. She spoke broken English so I didn't understand that she was going to the large zoo in Tokyo about twenty miles away on the train. As time passed and it was getting late in the day I became concerned they had not come home.

I went across the road and asked her parents if they knew where she was but they did not speak English at all. That was not a big help. It was almost dark when they returned home and I was so upset … no, I was scared. I didn't have God to call on and there was no way to contact them. Hubert was at the base and I had no transportation.

Needless to say that did not happen again. I did not think about thanking God then, but I do thank Him now that everything was alright. Kaiko was very apologetic.

In Japan, Debbie asked me take her to Sunday school every Sunday. When our tour of duty was over her Sunday school teacher gave her the three year pin for not missing a Sunday. She gave it to her a few weeks early because we were leaving.

We returned from Japan in 1958 and bought a new home right away, but it needed finishing touches as we could not get our furniture out of storage for a couple of weeks. The neighbors were so kind and helpful and loaned us mattresses. We also ate out. Our neighbors were great and we were friends for the years we lived there. Finally, our furniture was delivered. We lived between an Air Force Colonel and a Lieutenant, which made it a little awkward since Hubert was a Sergeant (and not allowed to be socially involved with them). However, we broke that rule and just didn't go on base together.

I was very happy with my home, family and all the things we were doing together. I thought we were doing very well in many ways because there was nothing lacking in our lives. However there was still an empty place inside me that didn't satisfy me, even with our new home in Savannah Georgia, along with all the other things we had including our great friends.

Debbie, our oldest daughter, always had a heart toward God. I give credit to my parents who planted a seed in her heart while we stayed with them during the time we were waiting for our orders to Japan. The girls had dozens of friends and the neighborhood was great. There was a dead end street and not a lot of traffic so the street was safe and I counted as many as 32 children on our patio one day.

Soon after arriving in Savannah, Georgia she found a group of children who were having Christian classes in their home. She came home one day to tell me about an Assembly of God woman who had invited her to go to church with her. She went with her as long as we lived in Savannah.

We moved from Savannah Georgia to Montgomery Alabama and opened a small business. We moved to Perry Street on the corner next to the Governor's mansion and Debbie soon became friends with the Governors daughter. Twice a week she would be invited to go to the mansion and play with their daughter. She has her way of getting involved, where she was.

The Lord really began to show me just how awful it would be for the rapture to take place and for me to be left behind. A fear gripped my heart and I lived in misery most of the time. If my dislike for Christians had not been so strong it would not have been that hard for me. But I didn't want to see anyone who looked like a Christian or who even went to church. To me they were all hypocrites.

That feeling first developed when the church I had attended about fifteen years earlier went through a very difficult time and there was a split that left many people disillusioned especially the younger Christians. That is the reason why now my heart grieves over any type of church trouble. Someone always gets hurt. I am trying to reach out to some people now that are no longer in church. Because of church problems they did not know how to handle, they dropped out. If you are one of that group, please give the church another chance.

Several months after I returned to the State of Alabama, I met an old friend named Pauline. I was on my way home as we met. We stopped our cars and talked awhile. It had been many years since I had seen her and one of the first things she told me was that she had accepted the Lord as her Savior. She didn't seem to be a threat to me because I did not realize just how changed she was, and after all, she had lived the same kind of life style as I had lived. She was in the same church as I was when it split.

The culmination was when she put my name in a prayer box at a Thursday morning prayer meeting at her church. Their prayers along with my parents' faithful prayers caused God to begin dealing with my sins in an even stronger way and I began to try to change on my own. I would lay aside everything that I thought was wrong but soon I would be doing the same things in an even more severe way.

I suppose God was showing me that it was not how good I could be but what He could do to change me. It was at this point that I really began to be fearful and I started begging God to help me. The fear that came during the Cuban crisis is when I finally accepted Christ. It was at that time that God began speaking to me about what He wanted me to do. I came to a place of desperation and I became willing to do anything to get back to God.

I actually thought I was losing my mind and that was possible with all the pressure from Satan who knew I was changing. He was trying to convince me that it was hopeless for me to be saved and that I had sinned too much. At the same time, God was applying quite a lot of pressure for me to change. It was a challenging place for a backslidden Pentecostal person, and it was almost more than I could bear since I had no intentions of changing. It took about a year before that day when the pressure of Satan began and God was calling me back.

That makes me know that God has the ability to change a person's mind. As I think about Paul who seemingly had no intentions of turning to Jesus, but when God sent a bolt of lightening he began to have second thoughts. It's also the same as Jonah who said that he would not go to Nineveh. God sent a whale to change his mind. Then there was

Nebuchadnezzar, whom God sent to the woods to live like an animal until He knew there was a Most High God who rules in the kingdom of man. According to Daniel 4:32, God can do anything!

CHAPTER 4

❋

Straight Paths to Victory

1961: God is so in tune to our lives and makes plans for them accordingly. At the time, He was drawing me by His spirit. He sent a young lady to visit me from the church that my daughter was attending. She was very convincing and I began to desire to know God. In a short span of time Reverend Billy Walker Jr who was a fiery and young Baptist minister, came in and forcefully hit the counter and said, *"Have you ever been born again?"* It frightened me so bad because I knew I was not born again but I tried to hide my fears. God was getting me ready for the change that was coming to my life, which happened like this:

It was on a cool fall day in 1962. The sun was shining,

the birds were happy and singing, but within my spirit it was very stormy and unsettled. My life was in shambles and my emotions were at a breaking point. Even though I had a wonderful marriage, two healthy, smart girls and the small restaurant we owned was doing well, I was very unhappy with my life.

Peace could not be found. Time and sin took its toll on my life and I was deceived and my thoughts seemed to be controlled by demonic powers. It seemed impossible to be forgiven because I was convinced that I had sinned against the Holy Spirit. Feeling hopeless, because I had been so hard and harsh against the church and God's people, I had no place to go and no one to whom I could turn.

As a result of these circumstances, it was a long, hard year for me. I read my Bible every night, even though I could not understand it very well. I was in such spiritual darkness and I was looking for help. Having a little spiritual insight, I prayed to seemingly no avail. That was the time when there was a threat of war with Cuba and a fear griped my heart that would not let go. Each time I heard a siren, I would cringe on the inside. I was afraid we would be attacked and I would be killed.

I was devastated knowing that I was not saved, and horrified at the thought of being eternally lost. I lived with this fear day and night for many months, which was damaging to both me and those around me, yet no one knew the battle that raged within me. Satan was holding on so tightly and God was drawing and pleading so tenderly. That was the conflict I was in, I was so intent on being saved, yet I was still in the clutches of Satan as he was so convincing that I had sinned too much to be forgiven.

God had a plan and as I sought for God in seeming hopelessness, a small portion of scripture came to my mind. Since I could not recall a single scripture that my dad had taught me during all of my formative years, the scripture that opened up to me was *"all things are possible with God."* I took hold of that word quickly and said to God, *"If that is true then you can save me."*

From that time on I had a new confidence in God's Word. Having been raised in a Christian home by parents who were ministers and totally involved in the work of God, I was not ignorant of the Bible even though it was hidden from me during my departure. As children, we were taught daily the ways of the Lord. Twice a day devotions were part of our life and we all gathered around our dad for Bible teaching and created a strong Christian atmosphere that I grew up in. By not living the way I should caused me to be sorrier for my sins.

In the midst of the turmoil God was calling me to that commitment I had left behind fifteen years earlier. I heeded that call about two o'clock that afternoon and God came into my life in such dramatic ways until my family and friends could not comprehend it. I was transformed by the power of God but not without making a choice. The question from God was, *"What would I do to be saved?"* (Not that we have to pay for our salvation). I was so tired of the spiritual darkness that surrounded me. I was ready to commit to anything, so I told Him I would give my home, family and all else I had because at all cost I wanted to escape eternal punishment.

At once, I began to experience the cool sunny day and I could now hear the birds sing, and experience the calm that comes after the storm. I had been born again. At my conversion all fear was gone and a new day dawned in my life that is still bright and more beautiful every day. It all began with dreams, visions and God speaking directly to me and that is the way He still contacts me.

God honored the consistent faithfulness in prayer of my parents as they gave themselves to train and teach their family. All my siblings have gone on to their eternal reward leaving with us with an assurance they were ready to meet their Maker. Only I remain, continuing to serve the Lord with my whole heart. I heard my dad pray every day at our devotional time that our family circle would not be broken in Heaven and as of now, that prayer has been answered.

Hubert was not all that ready for the change, so I had to be willing to accept anything that may happen to every area of my life. The way that God was presenting it to me it seemed that I just might lose everything, so I gave it all up to God and trusted Him to keep me secure whatever came my way. Those were very difficult months for me.

At this point, the miracles began to happen. First, God delivered me from a lying devil, which I told to go, which is a constant reminder that we do not have to walk around being influenced by the devil. That spirit would force me to tell a lie when the truth would have been best for me. I realized that we have very little control over the sin in our lives especially when we have once known the Lord and deliberately turn from him.

I turned from Him long ago, around 1946, when one day the young people I socialized with were going to a movie. For those who lived in the 1940's you know that Pentecostals did not ever go to movies and may I say they shouldn't today! However, values have changed so much in the church that many don't see anything wrong with it. I, along with King David in the Bible, choose not to allow my eyes to see evil intentionally nor allow my ears to hear vain things.

My First Miracle: I was awestruck at the miracle God did for me that week. Before this time, I was the leader in planning parties and fun times, which were not very pleasing to God. That Saturday night we had some of our so called friends coming over to view a home movie that was low standard and to have a party. However, after my conversion I knew I could no longer do the things I had been doing. I did not know how to handle that situation and I had not faced that problem before.

I knew that most anything I would do would upset my husband and the others. In fact, I had not told him that I had become a Christian. My question was, *"What can I do?"* After all, this had become a regular Saturday night event and my husband was not a Christian so he would not understand. In a helpless state of mind, I fell on my knees and asked God for help. I waited and there was seemingly no answer. Saturday night came and no one showed up for the party. That was over fifty-five years ago and not one of those people has ever called or come to my house again. There was no explanation, nor did my husband comment on the reason why.

From that time, I began to be drawn nearer to God by the Holy Spirit. I have developed a relationship with God so strong that we now discuss almost everything. I have learned how to talk to God and listen for His answer. Along with dreams and visions that have continued throughout my Christian journey, my life has been fulfilling. I am convinced that each person develops a communication method with God.

The Spirit's call to a higher place: God has brought me far beyond where I was and He has done more than I ever could have imagined. It has not been without many trials, some that were very severe. I wondered if I would make it. Troubles have taught me many things about God, as I bare my soul to God and depend on Him to bring me through. Experience has taught me how to put another person's soul in His hand and trust Him to save them, thus committing all types of situations to His care.

Because of His faithfulness to me, I believe I can place future needs and desires in His care. The Bible says, *"He is able to keep that which I have committed to Him against that day."* My heart now desires another level. A new desire needs to happen from time to time so my private time with Him will not become routine or just a habit. I must keep my time with him special. This kind of prayer life will help anyone to experience His grace, love and mercy during hard trials.

Hubert told me of a man who had a bleeding ulcer and was at the point of death. I became concerned for him and began to pray and I knew I needed to visit and pray for him. Hubert had gone to work and there was no way to contact him so I went to the phone book opened it and put my finger on a number and called it. The man's wife answered and when I inquired she told me his name and explained his condition.

I went to the hospital and they were working with him, and he had family there. I was not sure of what to do but asked God for an entrance. Shortly after I prayed everyone left the room and I went in. He was a small man but his stomach was huge. They said it was full of blood. I prayed and left. I inquired about him not long ago and he is still living and that was about 45 years ago.

1963: What Money? The business we had opened years before was now in jeopardy because the man who owned the business was selling the building. We were about to lose all of the money we had put into the inventory, so I asked my husband to go with me to my parents' house and tell my daddy about what was happening. I told him that my daddy would pray and God would help us. This happened just a short while before I was converted. We did go tell my dad and when we returned home I called the owner of the building and asked him if he would wait until we could sell the business part of it and he agreed to do that. We did not lose our money.

We had a period of time after selling our business that we could not find jobs because it was really hard at that point to find employment. Hubert went to other cities seeking work. Finally he was called to a state job where he had applied in the past. However, we had depleted our money and his beginning salary was small. It seemed as though we wouldn't make it but God had a plan to teach me how to make Him my source. God always seems to have a plan when things are going wrong. Prices were not like they are now in the 21st century. At that time I only had

$25.00 dollars per week for food and clothes and I tried to spend that very wisely.

Isaiah said, *"My thoughts are higher than your thoughts and my ways are higher than your ways."* That verse was made real to me one day. It was in the middle of our crisis that I was impressed by God to stop being so tight with my money and as always when God speaks we are to act upon His Word. When I went to the grocery store, I began choosing the items that were the best. The bill was much too high based upon what I had been previously spending but God had given me clear instructions.

At the end of the week when the money was usually gone, I still had the same amount as always. The next week, He spoke the same thing to me. He told me what to buy. There was a pair of expensive shoes that I liked so I bought them even though they were beyond my budget. By the end of the week I had the same amount of money as always. Some people would have told me that I should not have done that, but I knew what God had said. God never looks at your bank account or you wallet. His provisions come from another source.

The next week He said the same thing and let me know that I could have the 9x12 foot rug that I had wanted. I thought to myself, *"Now, this is too much."* Even though I thought that, I went by His Word and I bought it. At the end of the week, the money was the same amount that I always had. I did not ever run out. God taught me at that time that He was my source and He has plenty.

Let me quickly say, this should never be tried unless you have walked in the Spirit long enough to know it is definitely God speaking to you. That is the only way it will work. If you do it just because I did, it will not work because He was working a miracle for me.

1963: If it had not been for the Christian legacy my dad and mom left us, it would have been a much more difficult life but they did leave such wonderful legacy for the family. A short while after I received Christ, I was sitting at my dining room table looking through my dad's scrapbook where he had recorded most of his meetings and salvations along with many other rich Bible truths.

He began writing scriptures about two kingdoms, God's Kingdom and Satan's opposing kingdom. As I was reading his writings, the Spirit of the Lord came into the room in the form of a fog. I could not see anything but the Glory of God, and I said, *"Lord, I know there is a table and chairs in this room, but I can't see anything."*

I stayed in His Presence for a while. I believe it was there that He started me on a search of the two kingdoms, the Kingdom of God and the kingdom of Satan because I really wanted to know of what they consisted of. I am so much richer in knowledge because of that study, but that is when I began to experience the effects of both kingdoms. I was attacked in many ways all at once. God was preparing me for a journey that He knew would be on rough terrain.

I have tried to pattern my Christian walk after my dad because of his strong dedication to God and God's Word. As a very young child, I was aware of Dad's consistency in Bible reading not knowing that he was committing it to memory. It seemed he never sat down without reading his Bible I was told he read it through 46 times. My brother Paul told me recently that dad could quote all of the New Testament and the old if you would start him off on the chapters. I wonder if that will have anything to do with his duties in Heaven. That is amazing to me.

As he preached he would quote passages from the Bible from Genesis to Revelation but never without holding the Bible in his hand and waving his hankie. He carried a hankie because it was so hot without a fan or air conditioning. Once, the word got out that he was slinging some kind of power with his hankie that made people pass out, because as he preached people would fall in the Presence of God as many still do today in some of our meetings.

There was so much excitement, praising, whirling and dancing around. They were rejoicing over the fact they had been rescued from sin and were on the way to Heaven. That was especially prevalent when my dad would preach on the coming of Jesus and Heaven.

People realized from what they had been rescued. It

seems now that we are so accustomed to hearing about Heaven that we pay little attention to it. That could be because we have lost sight of the reality of an Eternity in Hell.

CHAPTER 5

❧

A New Life Begins

It was on the Sunday after my decision to follow Christ that I left the house to go to church even though I didn't know where it was located. I did not even know the name of the church or the denomination. I had put my complete trust in God and I asked Him to guide me. I found the church without a problem and that has been my church since that day. I believe the church is like my home and there is no need to go elsewhere if my church can supply the full gospel of Christ.

From the beginning of my walk with God my interest was all about prayer. As I entered the door I heard some ladies praying down stairs. It was a group of older ladies and my age level group was in another building. However this group of older ladies possessed the qualities for which I was looking. It was in that group that I received my spiritual training on how to pray for my family and how to give myself to God.

Those meetings led to a Thursday morning prayer meeting where earlier my name had been placed in the prayer box and had remained there until I accepted the Lord. The Word says, *"He that goeth forth weeping bearing precious seed will doubtless come again rejoicing bringing his sheaf's with him."* After that time, I gradually became involved in teaching, and hosting Bible studies and prayer groups, which I continued to do throughout most of my Christian life even to this day. Prayer is my life line. Without prayer we are like an un-watered plant. We cannot grow, bloom or bear fruit without it.

Handling Difficult Situations: My husband Hubert and I didn't seem to have a lot in common anymore. Satan began to try to convince me there were a few things I needed to do in order to maintain our marriage. (I am about to learn one of the tactics of the devil and the workings of the Holy Spirit.)

I had a difficult situation, so what was I to do. One of my friends and I agreed that we would go to a place that was similar to the places we frequented before my conversion. As we were sitting there talking, the Holy Spirit spoke clearly to my heart and said that He was leaving with or without me. Wow! What a shock, so I got up out of my chair at once and said to my husband, *"The Holy Spirit said He was leaving and I am going with Him. Do you want to come?"* It was amazing how swiftly all of the others got up and left with me. It was as though a fear of God was in that place. Often we don't realize how powerful the Holy Spirit can work in and through us as we are obedient to Him.

About a year later, my relationship with God began to have an effect on my marriage. The scriptures say, *"Light and darkness cannot dwell together."* I began to be challenged by Hubert (who was totally devastated by my total change) to stop some of my Christian activities which I had no intentions of doing. I had experienced enough of the life of sin and I wanted no part of it.

During one conversation, as I was being confronted with what I needed to do in order to stay in the marriage, I turned to God because the situation was so different from anything that I had ever experienced. Our relationship had been just about perfect before my decision for Christ. It was then the Holy Spirit became so real to me and with the kindness and consideration that only God can give.

I began to explain to my husband how much I loved him and how devastating it would be if he were to leave. However, I could not and would not denounce any part of God or His expectations of me. He was free to make his decision. Later he began to relax and said no more about me changing. He made the statement that he would never darken the door of that church I attended. However, it was not many months until, by the grace of God, he was attending that church. God had come to our rescue once again.

It is not always easy to comprehend what an unsaved loved one must experience when suddenly they find themselves with a dedicated Christian companion for the first time. I think it would be safe to say that they are as uncomfortable with your ways as you are with theirs. This causes misunderstanding and conflict on both sides.

At times, it seems that the Christian companion has little understanding or consideration for the unsaved mate. It seems that we don't realize the power we have and they don't have the same help from God. May the Lord help each one of us to have the wisdom necessary to understand our mates in tough situations. The unbelieving companion has the worst of the two kingdoms. They can't enjoy the pleasures of sin because of the saved loved one and conviction, and they can't have the blessings of the kingdom of God because they don't know God. Peter says that the unsaved are saved by the chaste conversation of the wife.

God was moving in many ways in my life. My faith was getting stronger. Sometimes the Lord takes us down a simple path until we are stronger in faith. Then He shows us His power through faith. An example is an incident I experienced with the window in the dining room that had been painted shut several times. I had tried many times to open it but to no avail.

As I was sitting in His Presence, I suddenly knew that God would open that window for me. The weather was hot and we had no air conditioner. We only had a window fan and I really needed the air so I walked over to the window without a doubt in my mind and it smoothly opened without effort on my part. Praise God.

In early 1964 God began to use me in the supernatural realm. I was answering the phone for a live radio program for our church. I was receiving many calls when God revealed something to me about a call that came in. Since I was a new Christian, God explained what He was saying to me and said *"I did not tell you that because I needed to share it with someone. I told you so you can do something about it."* That was the beginning of the gifts of words of wisdom and knowledge. Through the years, God has shared many things with me so I could, on his behalf and most of the time, be used as a secret agent.

Learning to Trust God: As I was learning about trusting God, one of the first things I learned was to tell Him my situation. I was in need of a job so I asked him to give me a job that would be the best for Him and me. And He did.

From that time on when I needed employment I just told Him my situation and someone would always come to me and ask me if I would like to work at a particular place, I never struggled over it as I knew it was right.

I realize that goes against some theology about people having a free will. I believe in both the power of God and free will. However like the song says, *"He will not compel you to go against your will, but he will make you willing to go."* Seems the song writer got hold of that truth. What God spoke to me that day was that He has thousands of ways to convince people to change just like He did me.

Strange things begin to happen one day at work. I entered into deep worship and then realized I had to get away from people because the Spirit of the Lord was so strong in my spirit I could not stand still. I was being watched so I went to the restroom to worship for a while. What a God we serve! At the same time I was experiencing the visible Glory of God. It happened while I was in one of the hardest trials of my life. It was later that I realized that God was preparing my spirit to deal with even harder times.

One day as I was leaving work the Lord told me to quit that job. Remember, when He takes one thing from you He has something better or a better way. Hubert and I were in a long period of recovery from the time we had sold our business and could not find a job anywhere. Our savings had been gone for a long time and we were selling some of our most cherished items just to live. My husband later began working at the State Health Department but his salary was about $60.00 short of what our bills were.

Although Hubert never wanted me to work, this was a time when I really needed to. However, obeying God, I went home and told Hubert I needed to quit. All he said was that he didn't know what we would do. I could tell that he was bothered but didn't say much. We didn't know God had already taken care of it. A raise came through for Hubert in the next few days that was equal to what my salary was. WOW, what a God! Please don't try this unless you know beyond any shadow of a doubt that it is God directing you.

A lady named Doris was a praying person and she, like most everyone else had many bad problems, but she had an unwavering faith in God. One day she called me concerned about her upstairs door that was open. It should not have been since they did not use the upstairs and no one had been in the house that she knew about. She was almost in a panic when she called and so we prayed together and when we finished she said, *"Wow!" I sure am glad that is over with"*, and her fears were gone and she was able to go upstairs and see if everything was alright.

At this point in my walk with God, I was the spiritual leader of my girls. I learned during that time even the church leaders did not understand what a difficult role that is for a mother. I would meet the girls in their bedrooms for a devotional time before they would leave for school.

I recall how disturbed I was when I was made aware that the Junior High School where they were going that year was not a good environment for the children. Drugs were now being introduced in the schools and a lot of immoral things were taking place which I never encountered when I was in school. I went to God about it. Immediately the scripture came to me that said, *"Where sin abounds Grace much more abounds."* It is awesome how comforting the Word of God can be when we are in a dilemma about something.

Experiencing Changes: The moral standards began to change drastically in the mid-fifties. When I returned from Japan and being in San Francisco, it was the first thing I noticed even though I was not a Christian at that time. It was obvious to me something had happened during the three years I had been in Japan. It seemed the government was not as strict on crime and moral standards were declining through the years (those of you who were not there at that time probably do not understand what I am saying).

They were saying you should not discipline your children. They made it a law that you could not spank your child. And those of you who know the Bible know this is not God's way at all. Scriptures say, *'Whip him with a rod he will not die, but you will save his soul from hell."* Discipline is a must with God. He also said, *"A child that is left to himself will bring the parents to shame"*, and if he does not discipline you, he doesn't love you.

As the law began to change, so did society. It seemed all of the younger generation began to take advantage of some of the rights that were put into effect at that time and using those rights to do bad things they could not do before. Then the doctrine of, *"if it feels good do it"* and *"if your parents punish you, report it to the authorities"* began to circulate in our pop culture.

Since the government stepped in, it has become more difficult for those who are trying to bring up their children in the right way to develop young adults that have standards of living that can help bring peace to the world. However, I knew that this time had to come to make way for the antichrist. I trust the ones who are reading this now will do everything possible in their generation to bring up young people, disciplining them without abuse, according to the Word of God.

CHAPTER 6

❦

God Will Make A Way

December 1962: My Dad whom I held in high esteem, became very ill and I seemed to be the only one who could stay with my Mama to help out. It was almost impossible for me to do that because of my own illness. I had chronic sinus infections for several years and they were so severe, that for a significant period of time my headaches were so bad, I could not function properly. I wanted to help my Mother but I could not stay out of bed. I prayed for healing for a long time and I did not receive an answer.

Then one day as I was thinking about what Oral Roberts said about receiving. I thought that I would try what he said about finding a point of contact. My point of contact was saying, when my feet touch the floor, I will be healed. I said to myself that I will NEVER have another headache as long as I live and it happened as I had spoken. That has now been fifty- seven years and God has honored what I spoke. According to Mark, *"If you say unto this mountain be thou removed and be cast into the sea it shall be done, and again you can have whatsoever you saith."*

Beginning as a new Christian, I patterned my life after my parents. Many days I would spend six to eight hours with God. Much of my life I could hardly distinguish my daily walk from my prayer time because I would be in intense prayer, praise and worship even when I was communicating with people. When I worked I would arise at 5:10 each morning and stay with God until time to go to work and then continue in His Presence most of the day.

Many times the Presence of God was so strong that I had to withdraw for a bit because my body can't stand that strong Presence for a long period of time. These are the times when I am renewed in the Spirit so I can make it through hard trials, abuse and testing. If I stay in God's Presence long enough when His Presence comes, it is like water on a duck's back, or like an eagle soaring above the storm. Problems cause such little stress or aggravation you hardly notice. What you feel is compassion for the person who is causing the problem or understanding the problem enough to continue on without frustration.

Did I make mistakes and fail during this time? Yes. Too many times to name yet I would get up and go again realizing if I did not rely on God for my every move I will surely fail in areas I try to handle myself. This has been a great asset in my ministry to others. If I had not ever failed how could I understand when others do?

On December 25, 1963 my dad went to be with his Lord and to receive his eternal reward. His death was so touching for all the family especially the grandchildren because his custom was to go to their house on their birthday, knock on the door and say, *"I came to see you on your birthday: Happy Birthday."* Then he would give them a gift. My brother David wrote a song about him. It was Christmas day when he died and David said, *"He must have entered the gates of that city and said to the Lord, "I came to see you on your birthday, Happy Birthday."* That was the title of the song he wrote.

Be as Wise as Serpents: When there is a strong desire to minister and little understanding from your mate, you need the wisdom of God to know what to do. It was little by little that God gave the wisdom and freedom to serve Him but not without some failures and bad decisions that caused problems in my marriage at that time.

Early in my relationship with God I decided that what seemed to be the normal Christian life was not enough for me. I determined to be all that I could be for God and His kingdom, so I began to read and study the Bible to find out how to live. I would spread my Bible and all of my reference books out on the table and search for God. This has lead to years of reading, studying, teaching and preaching the Word.

The knowledge of God's Word that I have acquired by reading it through many times (the New Testament far more than one hundred times) has not been disappointing to me. It has brought me through many hard trials and has been a guide to me when I did not know which way to turn. I was determined to minister, yet there was a stronger desire for my husband and children to be saved. That was something that would take the wisdom of God.

I found myself longing for a prayer partner. Ecclesiastes says that two are better than one. My daughters were in the church choir and practice was on Wednesday night after church, so the parents would wait for the young people who did not drive, to take them home. As I waited for my girls, I heard these words in my spirit, *"Marie will pray with you."* Without hesitation I went and asked her if she liked to pray. She said, *"Yes."*

I was a little surprised because she did not appear to have that kind of interest in me as a prayer partner. However, I went ahead and asked her if she was interested in an all day prayer meeting and to my surprise again she said, *"Yes."* That was the beginning of one of the strongest relationships both in the natural and in the spiritual.

For many years we prayed and studied the Bible all day once a week, then increased to twice a week most of the time. She became one of my best friends as well as prayer partners. One day she asked about the house next-door to me and asked me to let her know if it ever came up for sale. After a few days I begin to feel in my spirit that I should ask about that as well as the house across the street hoping that if it was for sale, she would tell me at that time.

I hesitated to directly approach her about her house as her husband had been recently brutally murdered. She did say that the house across the street was in bad condition but she was thinking about selling her house. I knew that was God that had led me to ask her that. I called Marie and asked her if she was still interested and she said yes. About a week later I felt led to call the lady again about her house and I did and she said, *"I'm ready to sell"*. Marie and Kenneth bought the house and that was the beginning of a very close friendship and spiritual partnership. We were frequently involved in prayer meetings.

Other ladies began to join us. God did many healings and miracles and I will write about them later. Marie became the co-host on the television show God called us to for seven years. She also did other ministries, including women's ministries. She was always there to assist in everything, and she was the most faithful person I have ever met. As time passed she found other things to do and my life took another direction also. I moved to another part of the city, but years later we once again became involved in ministry together.

God Never Gives Up: I led many souls to Christ during those years and mentored many who came into the kingdom after me. Some would think I knew so much, not knowing it was my aggressiveness and knowledge for God. During those days I met a family who became my good friends. We shared some of the same desires for God. Their three children, whose Dad was killed some years before in an auto accident, was very tolerant of our many prayer meetings.

One of the girls, Judy, had become involved in some of these prayer times. During one of the prayer meetings, she was bowing low on her knees in prayer. At that point I had a vision of a huge creature about six inches long, clinging to her back, even penetrating into her neck. We prayed for her but at this point we had not been Christians long enough to know how to set her free from the enemy who desired her very soul.

I believe her story will be a blessing to those who seem to be bound by Satan in some way. She loved the Lord and tried so hard to serve Him, but it would not be long until she got involved in sin. She was married to a minister's son who got saved and the two of them served the Lord for a short period of time. She was feeling empty and lonely, began to drink and everything went wrong.

Right before her middle child was born, her husband left her for another woman. This is when she started seeking God again. Her husband came back but before long, things went wrong again. This on and off relationship with God went on for many years and at times she would rededicate herself to God. She would have a glorious experience then, but within months she would be back to her old life. Needless to say she would become more sinful each time, because the scripture says that when a person has been saved and returns to their old ways the latter end of that person is worse than the first.

She is now back with God and seemingly established in Him. She came back to Him several years ago when she came to the end of herself and searched for help. God has brought her a long way since then. Judy is now a vital part of a ministry called, *The Healing Place*. Not many people know how to help the desperate and defeated people without experience but since she has been desperate so many times she is able to help. Her heart now goes out to these people.

1967 Mother's healing: My mother had a brain tumor that was untreatable. I began to intercede for her and one night I tossed and turned on my bed in intercessory prayer for her. Doctors had sent her home to die. She was informed that within three weeks she would begin to see webs before her eyes and then death would come.

As I prayed that night, God spoke to me about taking her a miracle. I asked the Lord how He would like for me to carry out His plan. My instructions were to take her the miracle and give her instructions on how to begin eating again. It had been quite a while since she could eat anything, but crackers. At that time we only had one car and my husband used it for his job all day, every day. That presented a problem, but God began to speak to my heart and let me know that all I needed to do was ask. I asked my husband if it was possible for me to have the car for a day and he said that I could. God had already gone before me and made a way. Oh! What a God!

On my way to her house that day, all I did was cleanse my heart and mind of anything that I was thinking and any plan that might hinder. By the time I arrived, my heart was ready. With my mother being sick for so many years with a tumor on her pituitary gland, it would be interesting to see how God would convince her to receive. However, as always, He had prepared her.

I was not polished in my methods of delivering God's messages, so I walked in and asked her to please sit down. I told her that I had a message from God for her and I proceeded to tell her that He had sent her a miracle. I told her that He was healing her brain tumor and that she was to start eating very slowly. I had no doubt about her receiving the miracle because God was in control. She received the miracle gladly and none of the things happened that the doctors had said would happen.

Years later when she began to have headaches, the doctor told her that the tumor was becoming active again. A spiritual anger arose in me. I defied those words in the name of the living God. A neurologist in my hometown examined her for two or three days and sent the tests off. A few days later he called me into the room and began to explain that an impossible thing had happened. The tumor had dried up to the size of a lady pea and could not cause her any problems. It was a mystery to him because she could not take the treatments that were necessary. James says, *"The prayer of faith shall save the sick and the Lord will raise him up."* She lived for several years and the brain tumor never bothered her again.

One day when she was cooking breakfast, she fell and broke her hip, went into shock and that is what caused her death. I sat in the hospital with her the last three days of her life although she could not communicate. On the third night she became very restless, groaning with every breath. I walked over to her bed and began to sing *"Amazing Grace"*. After awhile I stopped and she started groaning again so I started singing again and she relaxed.

That went on all night. I was so hoarse the next morning I could hardly speak. It was about five o'clock in the morning that I realized her breathing was slowing down. I called the nurse and the family but she was gone in a few minutes. I was relieved because it was not good for her to suffer as much as she was. God was with us in the process of her burial and I knew it was God's grace that carried us through.

1968: Choosing a mate for my girls was a personal thing for me and I had spent much time doing all I knew to do to prepare my girls for marriage. As most Mothers can, I can look back and almost grieve over some of the mistakes I made. Nevertheless, I was as faithful as I knew how to be for the task.

In the corner of our living room there was an old piano where I would play and sing to the Lord every day. It was almost like a retreat from the details of life. Many times I found new strength for my life and answers to prayers there as well as making new dedications to God. There, my two girls gathered around me and we began to pray for their future mates. We asked God for their protection and training as well as health.

It was an awesome time and Laura mentioned those times to me recently (She was relating a story about Rodger, her husband). It was about the same time we were praying that he and several others were in the hospital with spinal meningitis. Some of the guys did not live but Rodger recovered nicely and we all know that God surely kept him and brought them together.

He Will Sustain You: The Bible says that offences will come. If you haven't had offenses and are not having them now, then you will have them in the future. I am persuaded that offenses are the one thing in my life that brought me closer to God than any other trial.

God allowed a certain person to become my arch enemy (or so it seemed). They opposed me in every possible way they could. They slandered and criticized me publicly and privately. They also spoke down to me at all times.

God gave me such sadness of heart for them because I knew if they did not repent it would not be good for them on judgment day. I prayed for them many times. However, there were other times when I would become so weary because it was necessary for them to be in my presence and quite often. This situation tried me until God was finished teaching me. I am persuaded that if I had handled it better and the trial would not have lasted that long.

May I quickly say that I was not without fault when I would become overwhelmed by the poor treatment I received. I would retaliate sometimes which would only make things worse since I was not yet an overcomer. I would forget that we wrestle not against flesh and blood but against principalities and powers (Ephesians 6:12 KJV). It was at the end of their life about 25 years later when they said all was well with them and God. Praise God for His grace and mercy. I am looking forward to seeing them in

Heaven. David said in Psalm 21:2 KJV, *"Thou hast given him his heart's desire, and hath not withholden the request of his lips."* Again, it is not what a person does to you but it is how you respond to it that counts with God.

It was during these same troubled years there was always a prayer meeting at the church and my friend Connie would come from work on her lunch hour and pray. She was a true intercessor. One day the Spirit of the Lord came into that prayer room in one of the most powerful ways I had seen. After a long period of intense praying, most of us were just sitting and waiting in the Lord's Presence. Connie was under one of the tables, totally drunk in the Spirit. For those of you that don't know what that is, it is when the Holy Spirit comes so strong upon a person they have to surrender to Him. He takes control of them and takes them into another level of Glory and gives them a special blessing.

That is what happened to Connie that day. We finally got her out from under the table because we knew she was supposed to go to work. But she was so under the influence of the Holy Spirit that she could not walk or hardly stand. She started laughing and praising God. She was not concerned about anything of this life, only God.

We got her to the door and she said that she could drive, still laughing and crying at the same time. She finally made her way to the car. We were all concerned about her driving.

However we know God was with her. Later, her boss lady called me (she had once been a Pentecostal but had backed off from it) and wanted to know what was wrong. Connie was at the beauty shop where she worked, witnessing to people and was still drunk on the Spirit. The Bible says, *"Be not drunk on wine but be drunk on the spirit."*

A little later, her husband called and wanted to know what was wrong with her and I assured him that she was alright and that there was nothing to worry about. I am sure he did not understand what she was doing since these things are spiritually discerned. Shortly after her boss called and questioned her actions, she came to church with Connie and God answered my prayers and her friends had to help her out of the church.

The Bible says *"Be filled with my spirit and you shall be my witnesses"*. You can't be totally filled without witnessing to others and God then gives the increase. So many times of refreshing came that I will not mention them all in this book but the Lord will take you places beyond the realm of this life if you will seek Him and receive it.

CHAPTER 7

❧

Children

1968: My daughter, Debbie, was a real blessing to me with her caring ways, but as most teens do while they are growing up, they don't always make the right decisions in life. They have to have the proper guidance of their parents. Debbie was a wonderful Christian and she was involved in the youth programs at our church. However, as she was trying to help a peer at school, she became too attached to her for her own benefit.

She was walking home from school with her every day and the girl called her continually. She was doing things which I did not approve, so I was very troubled because I had experienced the trickery of the Devil. Knowing that He tries to get Christians to deviate from the truth, I began to call on God and I must confess that I was a bit concerned. As I was standing in front of my kitchen window one day crying out to God, I heard in my spirit the voice of God very clearly. It seemed that I heard it with my ears and it sounded like a rebuke for my unbelief and a promise combined.

He said, *"Why are you so concerned about one little girl when all the powers of Heaven are at your disposal"* I turned and pointed at the telephone saying *"You shall never ring again with a call from Faye."* Needless to say, she never called again proving God's Word to be true and that you can have whatsoever you say. May I hastily say it is only in the spiritual realm that this can be done and only if you are living according to God's Word to the best of your ability.

1972-73: My younger child, Laura, was also a joy. Both girls were exceptionally good girls. They were born again and involved with the church. However, Laura also had her times that she needed parental guidance. When she was seventeen she fell in love with a nice looking young man and became interested in him to the point of marriage. God spoke to both my husband and me this was not the one she was to marry.

One day while she was out running an errand for me, a call to intercessory prayer came to me so strongly that I fell to my knees in agony of spirit. I thought for sure something bad had happened to her but she came home shortly. When I inquired about her trip she said everything was fine but the Spirit doesn't lie and He had let me know that all was not well. I continued to inquire about what had happened and as she realized I knew something, she began to confess that she was at a friend's house planning a wedding.

Now that my husband was a Christian I had someone to agree with me in prayer. We went to another couple's house who attended our church to get them to agree with us in prayer. However, it is hard sometimes to leave things in God's hands so we tried to do all we could to help. Nothing we did seemed to work. I talked to the young man and told him how God had spoken to me about his future wife. He told me that she would be a great asset to his ministry and that did not go over very well but God eventually worked it out.

Laura went to Southeastern Bible College in Florida and when she was gone, I thought things would change. The young man never finished high school, so he could not go to college. Much to my surprise he got his G.E.D. and went to the same college Laura was attending. Knowing that God said that he was not the one for her, fear griped my heart because I was no longer able to keep an eye on the situation. They were out of my reach and free to see each other as often as they wanted. With every situation it seemed we had to learn that God could handle it without us being there. This young man was seemingly a good guy. We just knew he was not the right one for her.

A few weeks later the Holy Spirit called me to intercede again and I prayed and prayed until there was no strength left. I finally said to God, *"I need something tangible that I can see, in order to receive."* That day I had received a newsletter from David Wilkerson and it was by my bed. I picked it up and there was a picture on the cover of an angel holding the prison door open for Peter so he could go free. That picture spoke to my heart that God had answered my prayer and without another sign I received it from God.

I began to rejoice over the answer that I knew I would receive, and could I confess something just between you and me? My rejoicing turned into dancing and as I rejoiced and danced, the phone rang. It was Laura and this was what she said, *"Mama, this does not have anything to do with you, but while I was just sitting across the table from that young man, I began to think, I cannot spend the rest of my life with him and sit across the table from him every day."*

She broke up with him that day. This young man had a very hard time letting her go. He pursued her and Laura was so in love with him. The young man married a singer and he is now an evangelist. Later that year, Laura met the young man to whom she has been married for thirty two years. God said, *"All things are possible to him that believeth."* God has a plan for all of us. It is not always easy to wait for that plan.

1978: During the winter, I was seemingly alone for months with no prayer partners. I very seldom received a phone call, which was not normal for me so I stayed in prayer all during the day and evenings. After a few months I was feeling so alone (I was not working at that time which made it seem lonelier) I walked to my back window and looked at an apple tree just outside. It looked so barren and dead that I said *"God, I feel like that apple tree"* and God replied, *"The tree has to have the winter to kill off the bugs and the dormant time to prepare for the fruit bearing time and so did you."*

To my amazement, a few weeks later I looked at the apple tree and little leaves were sprouting on it. God spoke to me and said, *"It is also spring time in your life."* Much that I will write about next came after that experience. My life began to spring forth with activities and people that were outstanding to me.

Working for His kingdom: There was a chair in the corner of my living room where I would go to pray throughout the day. That's where I would encounter God when I needed Him. About 1978, during one of my prayer times, God gave me a vision of a large class and it began to branch out into smaller classes. By then I was aware that God was showing me something that I would be doing. I waited and about a year passed. I thought that each time I was asked to teach a class that was it.

Then one day the Sunday school superintendent stopped me in the hall and handed me a set of books and said, *"I want you to teach this class that the pastor is supposed to teach. The pastor is doing something else."* I knew that was the class God had shown me even before I knew what the subject was. I looked the books over and I felt someone else could teach it better because it was four books about training teachers and workers. The course would last a year and I couldn't help but be amazed. I could see how the other smaller classes would go out from that class. It was a class I did every year for the next seven years. That was one of the greatest blessings of my life.

CHAPTER 8

❋

Faith and Miracles

1980's: I contracted the shingles and when I was trying to recover from the disease I went back to work but was not very strong. As I was closing the beauty shop where I worked I had to stand on a box to turn off the lights. As I stepped up on the box, it turned over and hit my left ankle and broke it in two places. I was thrown against the wall and hit an outlet box, seriously injuring my right arm which took me off my feet for six weeks. I could not use my crutches and could not put any weight on my foot.

I was taking medication for pain not knowing I was allergic to it but I was aware that I was getting worse. I kept taking the medication until I couldn't eat and was dehydrated and very nauseated all the time. Thinking it was the shingles that were still making me sick I continued to take the pain medicine because the pain was severe. One day when I could no longer get out of bed and was almost past moving, Jesus stood by my bed.

He was speaking with something that I could not describe because it was most likely a spirit, which I believed later to be the death angel. He spoke to the being and then would look at me with a serious look. I could not hear Him speak but I could see His mouth moving. Then He was gone. I called out to Him and said, *"I have served you faithfully for all of these years and I deserve to know what you were saying."* I was a little surprised at my boldness with Him. However, I knew He loved me and I loved him enough to be real with Him.

At that point He came back and started talking with the spirit again the same way and then He looked at me and smiled. That was enough for me. Then He was gone. That night I was just laying there. I couldn't move and I began to feel my muscles and my nerves relaxing. I could feel all the unevenness in the bed and that was unusual. Then I realized something was happening to my body that was not normal.

At that point the spirit that talked with Jesus that afternoon came back and began to communicate with me but not verbally but through thoughts. It let me see all the things I had done in my life and all the beauty and blessings of Heaven. He reminded me that I had lived all of these years for that moment, so he asked, *"Do you want to go or stay here? The choice is yours."*

At that point I was not feeling any emotions so it was all facts and I thought about my daughter in North Carolina. She had called that afternoon and said to me, *"Don't you die until I can come down there."* I don't really know why she said that, but now I had to consider that and the question the spirit had asked. Not being moved by emotions, it made it hard to decide. Again the spirit said, *"If you want to go, just close your eyes and go to sleep, but if you want to stay, you will need to stay awake."*

I said, *"I hope I am not making a bad decision, but I will stay here."* I wondered for a long time if I had done the right thing because at the moment my thoughts were more spiritual than natural. As soon as I made my decision the muscles and nerves began to activate and I could feel them as they began to snap back.

Earlier that morning, Sharon, my prayer friend, had come over and cleaned my house. While she was there she came in the bedroom. Just before she left she placed a lollipop sucker on my bed and said, *"I am leaving this for you."* When my choice to live had been made, I remembered the lollipop. I could barely move, but I managed to get the lollipop. I used that to keep me awake because I was still very sleepy with a strange kind of sleepiness but I stayed awake and that was when I began to improve. I can now see reasons for me being here on this earth. I suppose Jesus helped me make that decision.

1981: Shortly after that experience, Sharon expressed to me how she had a desire to have a Bible study in her home. She asked me if I would teach it. We started the Bible study and I was taken aback when I realized that I had not brought my lesson plan. I realized God was the one who originally gave it to me and I was sure He had not forgotten it.

We prayed and I taught. I believe that I can say I did not miss a point. I was so anointed and I believe that God knew that day I needed Him. The Bible study turned out to be the most spiritual Bible study in which I had ever been involved. Sharon and the others there were ready for God to move in their lives and the Holy Spirit moved in such a sweet way. He seemed to hover over the group and we grew until we had to move to the church. The prayer meeting developed into a women's ministry which was very outstanding and many things were accomplished there.

Many years later others took charge of the ministry and I felt such void in my life because I was not busy for God. I walked the floor and called upon God. He began to talk to me about a *"Call to Worship"* meeting involving people from other churches. I did that several times and it went well. Then God had me change to an all ladies meeting called *"Women Encountering God"* which was an awesome thing to me. We had two of those meetings and many were filled with the Spirit. When I am not in some kind of ministry I seemingly don't progress. I was still teaching a Sunday school class and did a few other things but it was not as fulfilling as when I was in a prayer group and being involved in some kind of outreach ministry.

1982: Hubert's family was not Christians and after I accepted Christ they stayed away from me. Some were very strong against me but God in his wondrous ways arranged for me to be there just before their death and lead them to Jesus, even his seemingly hard hearted Dad.

My sister-in-law suffered before her death and Hubert went to New Mexico where they lived and talked to her about getting right with God. She was not at all friendly with me but he convinced her to call me from the nursing home. She called me about eleven o'clock that night, ready to be saved.

Hubert was like that. He would lead others to the final confession but did not think he knew how to pray with them. As far as I know, all of his family members were saved. His Mother was also just days from her death when Hubert led her to Jesus. I was with him and walked him through the final part. That is something that others did not know about him. He was not as public with his witnessing as most are.

This next experience is most outstanding and totally unbelievable. One day during my prayer time I had a vision of a television station, the set, the cameras and I knew the guest and the subject matter. I was the host of the show and the program title was *"The Bible and You."* Marie, who now lived next door to me, was my co-host so I hurried to her house and told her about my vision. We acted like Sarah when she heard the angel say she would have a child at ninety years old. We laughed. I soon forgot about the vision because I had never been inside a recording studio and I knew absolutely nothing about television productions other than what God had shown me in the vision.

It was about a year later that the Lord gave me the vision again and let me know it was no laughing matter. I asked Marie if she was ready and I also asked Mr. Stevenson if he would teach and he said he would.

The night after that I could not sleep and I had this urgent call to teach God's Word but I did not know where. I never related it to TV. The next morning at work (I am a beautician) one of my male customers came in for a haircut. He was one of the ministers in our church and he also worked at a local television station which I was not aware of at the time. I began to tell him about my sleepless night and how I had prayed most of the night about teaching God's Word. I told him that I did not know what to do but it was urgent.

His answer was, "Ruth, *why don't you teach on television?*" I was so awe stricken with his answer because no one other than me and Marie knew about my vision. My reply was filled with astonishment. I told him that I knew nothing about television and I did not know anyone with whom I could talk. I did not know at that point that he worked at a TV station. He said, *"I do. I will make you an appointment with the program manager."* Astonished is not a strong enough word for what I was experiencing, but at his word and God's Word. I kept the appointment.

All I knew to tell the manager was what I had seen in the vision. Her reply was, *"I wish everybody that wanted to start a program knew as much about it as you do."* I know that was the knowledge of God. She asked me how soon I could start and I told her the next week.

For about two years I did that program on prophecy along with Marie and prophecy teacher, P. Stephenson. God told me to change the title to *"Changing Scenes"* and do a variety show featuring people from all walks of life such as lawyers, the Governor's wife, horticulturists and many others. We had fashion shows, panel discussions and other things of public interest along with a segment of the program on Bible teaching. We taught subjects such as marriage, family and other subjects of interest with pastors, youth leaders and other church leaders.

In all, the programs ran for seven years. Nothing is

impossible with God. To me, I was the most unlikely person that God or man would choose for that work. After 7 years, God told me I wouldn't return to the TV studio. What I didn't know was that Marcus and Joni Lamb who were the station managers at that time were moving to Dallas, Texas to start a station there, which has now developed into a worldwide ministry second to none.

Working with Marcus and Joni Lamb was such a great experience. They were an outstanding young couple with a zeal and love for God that nothing and no man could stop. They did experience many trials but anyone who serves the Lord will suffer persecutions. Many of you know Marcus and Joni Lamb are now owners of Daystar television network. God always rewards our faithfulness.

Changes come: When God was finished with me at the TV station, God gave me a desire to teach on His Glory and the Feast of Israel. Some look for fluff but l look for facts. I sought out teachers who were factual such as P. Stephenson in our church or others who were sound in doctrine. I always prayed for God's direction in the books I read asking Him to set guard over my mind so I would not get into error. My mind became very important to me realizing that what you put in will eventually come out either in a lifestyle or words.

I looked for books such as Smith Wigglesworth, Watchman Nee, Paul Billsheimer, commentaries, dictionaries and exhaustive concordances. At that point I applied myself to know the Word of God for myself so I would not be led astray by those who just sound good with no substance or not altogether theologically correct. It was shortly after I began to teach I had familiarized myself with the nature of man and the fact that we are a three part being, body, soul and spirit.

It was then that I saw the importance for students to be familiar with that and to know why they feel and act certain ways. Knowing how to allow the Holy Spirit to control our emotions and to conquer the part of our nature that is out of control is the most important. And even into this day I still do refresher courses on that subject.

Vision of Rapture and After: The next phase of my ministry including dramas...

Sunday morning 1993: I was sitting on the third row in church just before service began when the Lord gave me a vision of the Rapture and things that would happen after the Rapture. It took just seconds and the Spirit let me know it was to be a play or an illustrated sermon of enormous capacity. It was an outline of the production. I had to fill in the details He gave me as I moved along and He also told me the people that would play each part. They all seemed to fit the part and at that moment when God was revealing this to me.

Rhonda came down the aisle and God spoke and said,

"She will be the bride." Was I excited? No. I had a job to do. I am too far along by now to have too many selfish emotions about a call from God. I stopped her and asked her to be the bride in a play I was going to present (and as no surprise to me) she said, *"Sure."*

From that day forward I began to write and research the scriptures and call ministers for information, also calling my prophecy teacher P. Stephenson for details. That was after I had spoken with my pastor about the possibility of using the church. He was in favor of the play in which I can say he always is when the Holy Spirit witnesses to him that it is from God. He was also a big help with information concerning the subject. The play covered the things that were going to happen at the Rapture and after the Rapture. It included the Second Coming of Christ as well as the Judgment Seat of Christ.

The family life center was set up to portray the Judgment Seat and the Marriage Supper of the Lamb, with a throne area with six winged Seraphim and four winged Cherubim. The table was set with a wedding cake and all the trimmings. The play ran two nights and there was at least one person who received Christ during Pastor's altar call and many were blessed. Not long after this play my husband became very ill. And he went to his eternal reward.

1994 HUBERT'S DEATH: He had a long and hard sickness. The next morning after his death I made my way to my chair where I did my interceding and prayers. That's where I encountered God. I told Him that I had seen women who lost their husbands and then made a mess out of their lives afterward. I asked Him that morning to preserve my life and keep me from making a mistake and God has kept me all the way. My heart has been totally turned to Him and I have sought Him diligently.

Many strange things happened in the days to come that no one could explain. There was a two-foot entrance wall going into the bedroom that had about 15 square mirrors on it that I had been trying to remove but it seemed impossible without breaking them so I just let them stay there. It was a day or two after Hubert's burial that about 8 of the mirrors fell off the wall at the same time. Most of the family was there and witnessed that. Another thing is about the night he died.

We were at the hospital for the doctor to pronounce Hubert dead and there was no one home. The checks he had placed on the table went missing. When we returned home I noticed the checks were gone and later I found them between some folded towels. Another thing was, the key that we usually left in the back door on the inside, suddenly fell out of the door, landing in the middle of the kitchen floor.

These things were always witnessed by someone. My family went through all of his chest of drawers to see if there was anything important that he might have put in there but nothing seemed to be there. A few days later I opened one of the drawers, moved a few pieces of paper and laying in a neat order all the way across the drawer was over seven thousand dollars. They were in small bundles of twenties with a copy of the contract for the cemetery lots I had purchased.

I can see him now as he chuckled and placed it there. I believe he appreciated the fact that I didn't want to upset him at that time of his life by approaching him about buying the lots. That was the first time I had done anything like that and I suppose I did not know how to cover my tracks. I was told not to wait as it would be too stressful but to have as much done as possible. Also, a clock I had given him many years before started running backward.

I never thought that such drastic change would come to my life. The extreme loneliness and frustration was so hard to cope with. It was about a week later that I realized my taste had changed along with my attitude. Both were the same as his had been when he was alive even though we were so different in every way.

My brother Paul visited me and my friend Doris was there that morning. As Paul spoke with me he said, *"Ruth, this is not you speaking. Something is not right."* A little later I was concerned so I called some friends to come anoint my house and pray. That was the end of the attitude change but until this day, I don't know what happened to me. I do know there are familiar spirits that sometimes try to harass people and I do believe that is what that was.

Many other things happened that I could not understand. During this time I began to ask God to cleanse my life of every impurity. I spent much time on making sure my every action and deed was approved of God. As I did this Satan came in some unexpected ways to try to get me to deviate from the Word. This was the most difficult thing I had faced such as losing interest in church, the Word and in many other ways. But thanks to God, He brought me through and has used me to help others who experienced the same thing.

I realized at the same time that some of the members of my family were being drawn away from the right path by Satan so I began a very long vigil of prayer for them.

During that vigil, I had another experience that was rather unusual for me. I had been reading in the Bible the story of Elisha where all that was left of the enemy was a valley of bones. On that night while I was reading and praying, I was lifted up to a place where I could look down into a valley and see two armies fighting. While I was wondering if what I was experiencing was really happening, I found myself back in my chair. I then felt God impressing me to read the story again. I was then lifted up over the same valley.

Suddenly, all I saw was dust and smoke and when it cleared there was only a residue left on the ground. Every enemy had been destroyed. I knew God was showing me that in prayer I had won the battle and once again, I was in my chair. It was in the early hours in the morning and I realized that I had been there all night toiling in prayer. The Bible refers to this as intercessory prayer. Intercessory prayer is when you intercede for someone else as it is very strong prayer.

1996 or 97 Fasting: My home for the past forty years was now empty. I had some prayer meetings and fellowship with friends after I moved, but there were only a few chairs there. God began to speak to my heart about searching for a closer place with Him through fasting and prayer. I decided to go to this house and take a mattress and some water and stay for three days. I just knew God wanted me to take my meal times and spend it reading the Bible and praying instead of eating. God says that His Word is meat and the Spirit is water. There was no food in the house and I did not take any with me. I set a time and date.

I began to go over to check on the place and to be alone with God and to talk to Him about my plans, telling Him that I would be there on a certain day at 8:30 to spend three days with Him. I was so looking forward to being with Him. I did that time after time until that day arrived. I was so excited that morning. You see I was going to find out what God wanted for me and not to ask for anything. I arrived with my bottle of oil to anoint the whole house and dedicate it to His service as I had done through the years. I went from room to room anointing every area of the house giving it to God for His pleasure for the next few days.

The Presence of God was so strong in that place. I believe that the dedication of that house that day caused me to get the price that I asked. The housing market was deteriorating at that point and it was almost certain that I would not get but half price for it. But I sold the house for the full price I was asking which gave me the funds to live for the next several years. I will take this opportunity to say that God has provided for me for many years. As I am faithful to Him, He is faithful to me. It is increasing and getting better as my life approaches the beginning of my eternal life.

Before when I tried to plan a prayer meeting on my own, I got very little results. But when God plans it, you can count on it doing what it was supposed to do. I had only told one person about what I had planned to do. She was a prayer partner at that time. To my amazement, there were nine people who came to pray. God set His approval on that time. It would take too long to tell about the next few days so I will just say it was awesome and that much was accomplished in lives. It was just the beginning of many prayer meetings where people were blessed, filled with the Holy Spirit, healed and strengthened as we moved to another house and then to the church.

1996: I was asked to teach a class where God took me deeper into prayer. God surely placed each student in that class to a group that was called to pray, as Marie (my assistant) and I taught on the Power and Glory of God. It was awesome how God moved in that class as each of us experienced the Presence and Glory of God. That was just the beginning of many other wonderful prayer groups and wonderful works of the Spirit.

God was really moving in an unusual manner. He placed some people in my life that were special to me. I was teaching a class and this group were all a great asset to the class and I was blessed by them being there. God opened the door in another city for us to go, teach and pray with a certain church that had a great desire for them to receive the Holy Spirit. The last night of the meeting, Linda asked if she could lead the altar service. As she did God moved and filled 18 people with the Holy Spirit.

This was not without an attack from the enemy. Without warning, one of the groups became fiercely jealous of me because they thought others were giving too much attention to me. They thought it should have been them receiving the attention. We must not be too judgmental of that person because it can happen to most anyone. Satan attacks and tries to use people who are the most committed to God.

The enemy can catch us off guard and start trying to use pride to cause confusion and stop the work of God.

I was so unaware of the whole thing until I was hit by Satan when I least expected it. I was in denial at first because I thought this could not be happening. This person seemed to be the most spiritual person in the class. She was seeking God and He was blessing and using her in many ways. This is the time we must be on guard because we are vulnerable. Satan does not like for us to seek God. In time I realized that I needed to face it. Even though I had fought the enemy before it seemed he came in a much different manner each time. This made it difficult for me to handle it like I should. It was obvious that Satan was moving against both of us so it lasted a very long time and I suffered many rebukes from that person. I'm wondering if I acted in love like I should have.

CHAPTER 9

❧

Ministry, Praise and Prayer

2002: Several years passed and I found myself in what I called a spiritual rut. God had called me years ago to be His "spare hand" which kept me on the move going from one ministry to another where I was needed. This led to conversations with Sharon about being dissatisfied with my present relationship with God. This led to us setting a special time to get together to seek God and within two weeks others heard and began to join us. That was the most awesome time of my life as I began to confess all of my slackness in service to Him and to express my displeasure with my life. We would gather each week, put some music on and just worship and seek God's heart. We could hardly wait for time for the prayer meeting.

Someone brought us a paper called, *"Soaking"* and that was what we were doing, just soaking in His Presence and getting closer to Him. God began to bring deliverance to each one as needed. One lady that had struggled for many years over some conflict in her life gave it all to Jesus one morning and she is still free today. Others began to prophesy and have visions, words of knowledge, messages in tongues and the interpretation.

Again we grew until my family room would no longer hold the people and we again moved to the church where we would meet and "soak" with some good worship music for an hour and then come together for whatever devotion God gave us for that day. Then we would put on our praise music and for the next hour or so we praised with banners, flags and small musical instruments.

During another prayer and worship time I began to see a beautiful garden. It had lots of plants, trees, flowers. In the middle of the garden and a little to the front, there was a large tree that towered above all the other trees. At first It had very green leaves and then it began to blossom and the wind was blowing softly enough to carry the fragrance out across the way and then it bared fruit. Another person said God was speaking to her that it was time for change and from that day things have been changing.

God has been doing new things. It was during these meetings that I was impressed by God to start searching my mind to see if my thinking was lining up with His Word and to my surprise, He began to reveal some things to me that were a hindrance to me and others. He began to show me where I had backed off from some of my strong teaching in order to gain favor with people.

I began to give my thoughts to the Lord, day after day and even if it took a while, I continued purging my thoughts. I repented of that and gave myself to God and today I am back and have been ever since then telling the truth even when it hurts. What God has helped me do already is wonderful! I am experiencing the peace that right thinking can give.

Focusing on God will help us to understand people and their faults better so we will not be as judgmental. It also helps us to be able to love the unloving. Spiritual growth always brings change and that is what God is bringing at this point. It is a little different due to some meetings by the pastor to examine our church to see what needed to change in some areas to be able to minister to the ever-changing society.

God begin to impress up me there was a need to help some of the parishioners of our church who are more unfortunate and needed our assistance. God is so faithful to reaffirm His plan for us. I am the founder and coordinator of a ministry called *"Sharing and Caring"*. This ministry consists of many areas of ministries such as helping the sick, visiting shut-ins, those who are less fortunate, as well as assisting those who need help of all kinds. At the same time, we were reaching out to bring the long time absentees back to church.

There were many other ministries others had been so faithful to do. I gave a complimentary dinner to show my appreciation to this group that worked so faithfully. As I sought God for a word of encouragement to these workers for those that had been so faithful, God gave me a beautiful vision to share with them of how He viewed their work. It went something like this.

I could see a house that had great curb appeal depicting the ministry of many people, consisting of many beds of all colors of flowers and much greenery, and the people passing by were amazed at the beauty. On the inside of the house was a variety of foods and areas of entertainment and relaxation. As I moved to the back yard it was breathtaking and there was beauty beyond expectation. The covered patio which seemed to be about twenty feet by thirty feet was adorned with huge ceramic pots of plants and flowers with plush seating areas on a ceramic tile floor of a variety of earth tones.

Beyond that to the left there was a swimming pool and a large water fall and fruit trees all over the yard with all kind for nourishing fruits to eat, as well as being beautiful to look at. On the left side of the patio was an area for the children with many neat places for them to play. I perceived the back yard to be about one hundred fifty feet by eighty feet.

I was so amazed at all of the different things I was experiencing when the Lord expressed to me that the front yard was the church. The ministers providing ministry to the people were the front yard workers. Inside the house was the ministry, preaching, singing, worshiping, etc. The inside of the house represented the many areas people could experience. Some were enjoying various things while others were eating, singing and laughing.

And even though some were bickering about menial things, all were family, deeply rooted in love.

The back yard represented the outreach ministry about which I was praying. He called these people *"back yard workers"* and began to explain these were people who would serve Him without a lot of recognition or praise. The work they were doing would provide love, comfort, nourishment, refreshment and happiness. Great will be their reward in Heaven.

CHAPTER 10

❧

Ministry, Praise, and Prayer

Prayer group May, 19, 2004: Our spiritual lives have to be checked out quite frequently because the god of this world is always trying to get our attention. At that point something has to be done to get our spiritual life moving again. Sharon and I were once again in that place, dissatisfied with our present relationship with God. This led to us setting a special time to get together at the church to seek God and within two weeks others heard and began to join us.

What a time we had at the Wednesday morning prayer meetings with all the instruments that Sharon and I bought so each one would have something in their hand to praise with as we played praise music and danced like Miriam danced. We also had special gatherings and featured the shofar. There were many other things God prompted us to do.

Sharon had an interest in prayer cloths and handkerchiefs for quite some time. She was impressed with Vestal Goodman's hankie. A visiting minister told about a woman who wanted to sing a special and she waved her hankies and said, *"Got the devil by the tail on a downhill trod, yippee yew yea hippie yew yo."*

This just stirred Sharon's interest in prayer hankies. She asked Marie to put lace around it. She loved it and wanted everyone to have one so she bought some to have lace put on them but God had other plans. Instead of the hankies becoming something to cry into, they became something to minister to those with burdens. That is what she has been faithful to do even though it has not been easy.

Several scriptures speak of using cloth as a *"connection to God's power."* Acts 19:12 says, *"And God gave Paul the power to do unusual miracles, so that even when his handkerchief or parts of his clothing were placed upon sick people, they were healed, and any demons within them came out."*

The women with the issue of blood touched the *hem of His* (Jesus) *garment.* I heard of a minister who went to a small town to run a revival and he stayed with some people who had to let him sleep in their bed. When he was leaving the wife told the evangelist that her husband was not saved and asked what she could do. He said, *"Don't change the sheets."* That night the husband woke up his wife and wanted to be saved. Who knows what God will do with these cloths since so many have prayed over them and anointed them. We have heard of many healings and deliverances.

In June 2006, I had a dream or a night vision that caused me to go into intercessory prayer for days and call on God to give us a workable plan for our loved ones to be saved. I dreamed the Rapture took place and as we arrived in Heaven, I saw a round white cloud over a small, what looked like an Island, and I thought, *"This is the Glory of God."* Entering, I saw all these people that I knew. However, I did not see faces or know their names. I wondered why it was so small and so few people.

There was a long table filled with food that was outstanding in size and quality and people were eating but I was not happy like I should have been. As I looked around, I was thinking there are no more than two hundred fifty people here. I walked over to a table and sat down. The Lord came over and sat down in front of me. I was amazed, but I asked Him, *"May I ask a question,"* and He said, *"Sure."* I asked Him where the others were. I was so upset when He sadly shook His head and said, *"I just could not let them in."* He said this three times. *"I just could not let them in."*

I asked if they could come later. I was becoming very

upset at this point, because He said, *"No, this is it."* As I began to cry and ask again if this was final and he said, *"Yes."* Then I thought, *"He will wipe away my tears."* When I woke up, He began to show me what the dream was about. He told me that it was not about Heaven and it was not about me. Then I realized that it was about our church. That was why it was so small and so few people. The cloud shows His Glory is on our church. The food represented the Word of God that we are privileged to hear, and I believe His countenance was saying to us that He cares about our loved ones who are not in His Kingdom. But there are still a few that's holding out faithful.

At times we recognize a situation is of Satan and at other times we seem to think it is the person we are fighting. Ephesians 6:13 KJV says, "For we wrestle not against flesh and blood, but against principalities, against powers, against the rulers of the darkness of this world, against spiritual wickedness in high places." I began to pray and search my own heart because in a time like that we can be tricked into thinking we are without fault. We need to know if we did anything to give the Devil an inroad to our lives.

As I prayed for them and for myself God worked it out. I asked God for their success in ministry and blessing on them especially the blessing of being able to see they were being tricked by the enemy. My prayer was that she would be hindered in the work for our Lord. Thanks to God that He will do anything we can believe Him for, but it will not be possible to believe until all things are right in your own heart. When we are willing to admit our own faults, deal with them through prayer and faith, it is then we have overcoming

CHAPTER 11

❧

Attitudes and Motives

As we move toward God, there are two important parts of our lives we should commit to the Holy Spirit. That is our emotions and attitude. They can cause your good works to be either rewarded or disregarded by God.

I think about three wonderful teachers that found themselves in a hurtful situation. The pastor needed three Sunday school rooms for other things he was planning. The rooms the teachers had taught in for many years meant their classes were going to be dissolved. Two of the teachers were very hurt and offended (even to the point that one of them left the church). The other stayed but suffered hurt for a long time. Later, that person had their class restored to them.

The third one, knowing they were called of God, found a place of prayer and surrendered to God and the leadership, yet claiming the will of God as teacher of that class. Later that day, the Sunday school superintendent came to that third teacher and said, *"I feel like you should keep your class."* It seems that teacher certainly had a good attitude and the right motive.

At times like these, you should examine yourself to see why you are doing the thing God has called you to do and if so, do you have the right attitude and motive? Is it your class or are you teaching for the Lord? If you are teaching for God, He will vindicate you. If not, then you should just let it go and start asking God to use you where He wants you. The heart is what God looks at, not the emotions or how your emotions change. Surrender to God because if we do not surrender we end up losing.

I discovered this while I was experiencing a very hard and long trial. The choir was singing the song *"He Loves Me"* and during that song God made me aware that He really did love me. But uncomfortable things had to happen in life to help develop character and strengthen our faith and confidence in Him and that was something I needed at that time.

In Watchman Nee's book *The Release of the Spirit,* he says if you are hurt or upset over something that someone says or does, it is something wrong in you that caused the hurt. If all is right with you and God you will only feel compassion for the person who has wronged you. I do believe that it is expedient for us to keep check on all of our emotions.

CHAPTER 12

❧

Hiding Place

I am learning now what it means to be hidden with Christ in God. I had a vague understanding of it before, but recently, He has let me see some of the meaning of this. I have often wondered why this has happened and some of you may be wondering why, when you do something for which other people receive the credit. Or maybe someone would do the same thing you are doing and they were praised and rewarded and it was like you had done nothing or that what you had done was foolish. Nevertheless, they received and you did not.

Because of this, one day as I was pondering in my heart if I was doing my service to God in the wrong way, God spoke to my heart and said, *"They can't see you because you are hidden in me and the work I have sent you to do will be accomplished."* That was a comfort to me because I want what I do to count for Jesus and for it never to be done for vain glory or self elevation. I never want my work to be done for the wrong motive and whether or not anyone sees it, is up to God. I just want to make sure I am doing it right and that He sees it.

1999: Having retired from my job as a beautician, someone asked me what are you going to do now and I said, *"I'm going to work at First Assembly."* That was the first time I had thought that. I am thinking that was a revelation from God. I started my job at First Assembly of God where I worked for almost nine years. It has been a pleasure working with so many wonderful people and ministers. They have been such a blessing to me.

It was about a year after I went to work there that God impressed me to minster to His people in several areas. I began that work in 2,000. The ministry called *Sharing and Caring* consists of many outreach ministries that will meet almost every need our people have. It has been such delight to be able to minister to so many hurting people.

Many members of the church volunteered to take different outreach ministries and I believe I have now, after seven years, fulfilled my part of the ministry as many capable people are now being led to continue with their work.

As I consider all of the different ministries God has used me in and how each ministry would last for seven years. I am waiting to see what God will do in the *Sharing and Caring* ministries. It is not only fulfilling but also exciting to work in the Kingdom of God. I want to serve in whatever capacity God has for me until He comes or calls me home.

It seems as though people are not aware of my talents and abilities. After all, what friend or leader would have chosen me to produce and host a television program for seven years? Or many of the other things that I certainly did not think I was qualified to do. But when I would tell God that He would always reply, *"That is why I have chosen you. The others know by the book, you will have to depend on me. That way I will be able to accomplish what I want to do."*

I was told that when He called me to teach the new convert class. And I told Him again about others that would be so good at this or that and also the teachers training course I taught for seven years. I just follow the Holy Spirit like the song writer says, *"God knows the way through the wilderness, and ALL YOU HAVE TO DO IS FOLLOW."* What a lesson.

Along with all the other things God did for me, He gave me the ability to understand people, leaders and pastors that could not see what God did in me. For those who could see became very jealous and treated me with disrespect and tried to push me aside. But God helped me to have a forgiving heart and taught me how to pray for them to be able to accomplish what they could for God. He did not want me to expect them to be perfect.

God told at times to watch as He took several people who did not treat me right to move them to other areas of ministry. God required me to always forgive them so they would not be hindered in the ministry. The scriptures say, *"Whose soever sins ye remit they are remitted unto them and whose soever sins ye retain, they are retained"* which to me made it very important to forgive those who truly do you wrong.

CHAPTER 13

❧

Green Berets

As I have examined the pattern of my life to see how God has led me. I noticed that I go into a situation either in my life or the life of others and as soon as God had taken care of the problem, I would be moved on to another person or demonic attack in a life. As I enquired of God about this, I began to understand that I was a Green Beret in His army. Some truths began to unfold as I thought on that topic, looking at the different types of service we have each been given by God.

We see David who was a warrior and Solomon who was more of a peacemaker. God told David he could not build the temple because he was a warrior. Then we have those who carried the ark and they were priests. That is what God was trying to relate to me that I am of the group who takes care of the skirmishes and short battles, not a long drawn out war where they have the front liners and then those who come up behind. I am more of a one who goes before and takes out the Special Forces that are doing a specific task such as those machine gun nests the enemy sets up.

God moves where there is faith. That is why some things are taken care of while others are not and besides, faith there is the perfect will of God to consider when we ask for His will, it may turn out different from what we desire. Plus, people occasionally do things that bring consequences and since we don't understand that, we often don't know how to pray correctly. We have to face the fact that sometimes we just miss it.

Eye problems: In 1992 I had to have glaucoma surgery on both eyes which later turned out very well. It was a normal day of work and I was preparing for my first customer when I began to see some movement out of the corner of my eye which continued all day and moved toward the center of my eye. I made an appointment with the ophthalmologist but by the time I got there what now looked like a cloud had moved to the center of my eye and I could not see out of that eye at all. The Doctor diagnosed it as Ischemic optical neuropathy.

I was so devastated when about a year later I saw signs of it starting in the other eye. I immediately called Rodger, my son in law in Georgia, to pray for me. We had devotions together for about a year while I lived downstairs from them. He would come down each morning with his Bible. We prayed together and the movement stopped and did not move to the center of my eye like the other eye did. I have been so thankful to God ever since for the sight I have left. it has been a long, hard journey adjusting.

I went to the same ophthalmologist as before and he said I was fortunate that it was NOT nearly as bad as the other eye. I have the vision to do anything I want to. All Glory to God. However, I was diagnosed with a bad cataract so for a long time I could not see to drive (especially at night). It was a hard decision for me to make to have the surgery because I only had one eye and I sure did not want to be totally blind. However it turned out fine and I could see so much better (I feel so blessed). I would like to just stop and say, I have the best son in laws a mother could have. God bless them for their love and consideration for me.

CHAPTER 14

❧

A Day of Sadness and Victory

It was a day like any other day when my daughter Debbie called me about a lump she found in her breast. We thought it was some scar tissue where she had surgery years ago. However, when she went to the doctor for tests it turned out to be cancer. A few weeks later she had surgery. There were some cancer cells in her lymph nodes so they started her on treatments that were very painful and caused a lot of nausea.

It has been several weeks now and much prayer has gone up to God (which seems to be working). She did not have the pain and nausea she had before, only a little weakness which I believe will also be healed in time. I think of the song, *"Whose report will you believe. I will believe the report of the Lord."*

On Sunday November 20, she gave her testimony which blessed the class. She told of a time within the last year when she and Leo went to the altar to pray and God gave her a spiritual refreshing that was life changing. On the fourth treatment she became allergic to the chemo. When it was time for her fifth treatment, she was concerned about what might happen but God was there all the time.

I had shared this with others a couple of times and it has been so strong on my mind. I kept thinking of a little song that said, *"Accentuate the positive, eliminate the negative, latch on the affirmative and don't mess with mister in between."* The morning of the fifth treatment, she walked in and on the bulletin board it said, *"Accentuate the Positive"*. It witnessed peace to her heart. The Word says to let every word be established by 2 to 3 witnesses.

God did something like that for her when they bought their first house and she was not sure it was the right one. I had been telling her little daughter the story of the secret garden and told her the back yard was a perfect place for her to have one and she was excited. The next time we went to the house to look at it again she opened the closet door and on the shelf was a card that said, *The Secret Garden*, which gave her peace about buying the house.

A word to my family: In closing this leaf of my life I

must leave this last word, in hope that it will spark a new desire in my family to know God, which is the richest life anyone can know. Knowledge of God is acquired by first getting to know Him as Redeemer and Friend, learning the Word by reading, hearing and developing a personal relationship with Him through a consistent prayer life.

Before I became a Christian I thought that I would never have fun or enjoy life again if I gave my life to the Lord. I didn't know at the time that real joy, happiness and a totally fulfilled life comes after you get to know God. Joy and real fun does not come in a bottle, drugs or any other substitute for peace. That is what the devil uses to give a temporary high. God gives a permanent high when He comes into your life and the more you give your life to Him the happier you become.

I am not trying to say there will never be great times of trouble. There most certainly will be trouble but He gives peace and joy in times of trouble. God said He would deliver us out of them all. He doesn't keep us from trouble, He takes us through them because it is in those times of devastating situations that He becomes more real to us and we get to know Him better as we see how He helps us. You would have the same problems without knowing God but with no help or peace. The Bible says that we learn obedience by suffering.

It is not enough for me to just go to Heaven. It will not

be good enough until every member of my family, every in law and all that is connected to me in any way reaches that same goal. Then I will be satisfied. That is how I live my life and that reason only. Nothing else is held dear to me.

Places I have lived during my sojourn on this earth.

I was born in Lewistown Pennsylvania in 1930, moved to Clanton Alabama near Pools Cross Road. Soon after that, I remember living at the Miller dairy farm when I was age 3 to 6. After that, we moved to Pletcher, Alabama near Maplesville in 1937. Then not too far from there, we moved near Pools Cross Road, and then to the Johnson house near Deatsville and before long, we moved near the airport in Clanton, to 12th Avenue North.

I moved to Dallas Texas in 1946, then back to Clanton in 1948. I moved to Birmingham in 1950, then back to Clanton in 1952 and on to Montgomery Alabama to Sarah Street, then to Miller Street in 1955. Next, I moved to Tachikawa, Japan, then to Savannah, Georgia in 1958. Then, I moved back to Montgomery to Court Street next door to the Governor's mansion, and then moved to Miller Street, across the street from the school.

In Montgomery in 1961, I moved to Garden Street, then in 1963 to Harmon Street, then to Locust Street in 1965, Harrison Road in 1995 to Promenade Apartments in 1997 and to Salinas Court in 1998. I then moved to Harrison Road, then to Bell Gables, then to Sylvest Drive in January

2008. Perhaps move from here to my real home, to move no more.

A Historical Day: November 5, 2008 was a historical day. A new President was elected, the first black President of the USA. I pray for him that he and the leaders of America will allow God to give them wisdom to lead our country during these troubled times.

The economy is looking grim and moral standards are declining rapidly beyond comprehension. At this point in history, our world is reeling and rocking spiritually with seemingly no thought of God except by the Christians. We need God more than ever during my life time. Election is over and things are moving in a troubling direction but God is still in control.

One more path

It is March 2009 and the leader of the Wednesday morning Bible study retired from teaching the class and asked me to take charge of it. I was very surprised because she had done a great job for quite some time now but she felt it was time for a change. She is still very much a part of the class. I really appreciate her walk with God.

As I began to teach, the Lord gave me a special love and concern for the people who live in these apartments. Some are sick and don't drive and because of that I began to desire to provide something for them at this complex. Beginning May 3, 2009, I was inspired by God to begin a church service on Sunday at 3:00 pm. Pastors from around the city have committed to come and minister, along with musicians and singers. God always has someone ready to do His work.

I believe this is the call to serve I was feeling earlier. It always comes when and how you least expect it. That is what I call walking in His will and not knowing what tomorrow holds, still being content to do whatever opens up for you to do. Not everyone understands the walk where there is such contentment by both walking in the Spirit and walking in His will. One hour you may be called to intercessory prayer and the next hour to go sit with a cancer patient or take a meal to someone, doing whatever is at hand for God's Kingdom.

Friends that made my life much more complete include: Connie, with whom I have had great spiritual fellowship. She is a true friend. I worked for her in the 1970's when she owned a beauty shop. She is a true Christian that has stood for the salvation of her relatives and has seen many converted to Christ that seemed impossible. She never took no for an answer when it came to her husband's salvation. Her love for him enabled her to pray tirelessly for him through many long years. She would not allow anybody to say negative words about him.

We have attended many prayer meetings together and she has put forth every effort to be at many of them as she could. I have been impressed with her steadfast life for years. Even in the midst of many storms of life I have watched her worship God and dance with all of her might before Him in praise. In late 2009 God found a way to get to her husbands' heart and he surrendered to God. He seemed to have respect for God all along.

Jerri: It was in the late 60's when I met her. She was in the Methodist church. At that time, her daughter Sidney was involved in a charismatic church and when Jerri and I met she was already interested in the baptism in Holy Spirit.

That was the beginning of a marvelous relationship and she was a strong influence on her husband and her other daughter, Jena. She and I have been traveling buddies and prayer partners and she has been there through the years. At times we would just go somewhere for lunch or dinner or even to the mountains or some shopping mall. We have a solid relationship that lasts even when we don't see each other for a while. We just pick up where we left off and go again.

Britani: What a great experience. She desired to move to Montgomery and it seemed to be out of her reach. I was considering having someone move in with me and it came together. She was a pleasant person and could cook. Wow, that was what I liked. Time moved on. Her boyfriend Justin is a very good musician and teaches other young people music which I immeasurably enjoy.

He is the son of our minister of music, a very polite gentleman with a great touch of God on his ministry. He would come over for dinner and maybe after a ball game. Justin came early one evening and cooked spaghetti that was yummy. Now, there is not one cook but two. Wow! That is great because cooking is not the most enjoyable thing for me. These two young and talented people were a delight to my life. Britani was eager to learn and I am eager to teach so that worked well.

The most precious thing to me would be in the late evenings when I was sitting in my private place in what I call my "prayer chair". She would come in for an evening visit where she knew she was always welcome. She would grab a pillow, lay on the floor at my feet and listen to me. I helped show her the way to be a good Christian, a good companion when she marries and some of the more deep things of God that was a great highlight of my life. Thanks to Britani.

The house where we lived sold and we had to move. We were both devastated but God had another plan and we both accepted it.

About that time another young lady named Jandalyn and I began to enjoy talking about the Lord and praying together. She had just returned from Rhema Bible College and had been involved in the previous prayer meeting Sharon and I was hosting before she went to Oklahoma. She would say, *"I have a song"*, and she sang *"I don't need nobody but Jesus"*.

She began singing in the church choir and that was the song that the congregation seemed to like best. Later she began to come home with me from a Saturday night prayer meeting where we would eat, talk about the Lord and some of life's situations, laugh and just enjoy the Lord's Presence.

Those were my two newest friends now I have already mentioned Pauline, Marie, Jeannie and Doris. I would like to say a special recognition for Dr. Jacobson. She has been there to share her expertise in many ways. Her prayer life has been a blessing.

Today is Christmas 2008. Last night, the family spent time at the Church café, having dinner and giving gifts to each other. This morning we met at a restaurant to have breakfast together. What a joy to be with family. Only three of my great grandchildren were there this morning but all but two were there last night. Jennifer is my granddaughter who is now carrying my seventh great grandchild. They live in Reno, Nevada and could not be here. Seth is her husband and they will be coming to see us sometime this coming year.

New church: We were all so excited and joyful on

that Easter morning. We all tracked mud into the church because of the rain but that was just a minor setback. The church was not completely finished. We had all worked so hard to be there by Easter. We scrape cement out from between the cement blocks and did a lot of cleaning up working as one. I cleaned bathrooms, buffed floors and did whatever was needed.

My girls were involved also, as well as being in the youth choir and other ministries. It has been great with wonderful years even though we have gone through some difficult situations I had some of my hardest trials during that time. The good has always outweighed the bad.

1996: I was asked to teach a class where God took me deeper into prayer. God surely placed each student in that class. This was a group that was called to pray, as Marie (my assistant) and I taught on the Power and Glory of God. It was awesome how God moved in that class as each of us experienced the Presence and Glory of God. That was just the beginning of many other wonderful prayer groups and wonderful works of the Spirit.

Around 2014: Pastor Greg is our new pastor. Reverend Jones was our pastor for 24 years and he brought peace to the church and did a great work while he was there. I feel like he laid a solid spiritual foundation with the Word of God that will be easy for Pastor Greg to build on. We have been so blessed to have these great men as our leaders.

Even though we are seeing a change now in the administration of the church, the Spirit is still moving and I believe we are steadily increasing both in numbers and in spirit. Pastor Greg has started a quarterly outreach ministry and it seems to be quite successful. He takes a group and visits the sick and shut-in's showing them we care. Pastor Jim takes his group and visits a retirement home or assisted living facility.

The youth pastor Jimmy, holds a special meeting in the youth room while the administrator takes his group to the streets to minister. Others help bag groceries, wash windshields and do other things to show the public that we are here and that we care.

Saundra does a great job ministering to the children and for the last three times I have led the intercessory prayer in the sanctuary. What a great time we have had with people who have a heart to pray, as we call out each ministry to ask God to crown their efforts with His Glory.

Other times pastor has special fellowships to encourage people outside our church to come inside and be a part. I am excited to see what the future holds for our church. The church has been the center of my spiritual life as it is a safe haven for me and my family over the last fifty five years and has prepared me for the next phase of my life.

I'll try to make it clear the differences between what I experienced with God during my illness, what I have learned through consistent study, prayer, and serving God over the years. Be aware that nothing is easy when you are working for God. We have an enemy to fight all along the way. A good scripture to put into practice during your walk with God is Nehemiah 4:17, which says to do your work with one hand while having a sword in the other hand.

We never know what tomorrow holds, March 2012: I was going about my business serving the Lord and that evening I had been to a meeting that God had called me to. The next morning about 3:30 I was awakened and I tried to move my left hand. It felt like somebody had tied it down. After trying to move it for awhile, I realized that I had a stroke.

God helped me to get in touch with someone. I found a shoe and started beating on the wall, someone heard me, and called an ambulance. I didn't know if anyone in my family knew what happened to me or not. I felt alone in the ambulance. I told the Lord. *"It's just you and here and I want to give everything to you and you have your way with me."*

Within a few weeks I was up walking with a walker just around the house when an accident happened. I fell and broke my heel, which caused a setback. However in a few weeks I was walking again around the house with the walker when another accident happened. I fell and broke the other hip. That's when I lost the big muscle in my left leg. That caused me to not have any balance on that side.

From that time on I have not been able to walk very far, even with the walker.

I remembered a comment that a minister made during his sermon many years before and he said when the Lord tells you to do something, to not let your body tell you what to do. I have remembered that through the years. I've asked God to use me every way He could. I didn't want to slow down even though I was very sick most of the time from the effects of the stroke. I was not capable of doing very much at all.

However, I have continued to teach the Bible study in the apartment complex where I live. I've returned to my Sunday school class a little later and then I started a Bible study in my home. I was involved in three ministries plus I did a significant amount of counseling. This has continued through the last seven years. During those years I've spent most of my time studying God's Word seeking a closer relationship with Him, trying to get to know Him better and asking Him to use me everywhere.

I do not want to leave one thing undone when I leave this world. I asked Him one day, *"When are you going to take me home?"*, and he said, *"When you get your work done then you can come home."* Evidently, I'm not done yet.

The remainder of my story is life-changing and one that has brought me to a place in God that I did not know existed. I could not have reached that place without the suffering, without the time I spent with Him, without the prayers that I have prayed seeking a better relationship with Him and without doing all the things that I did during this seven year period.

That has brought me to a place where God was going to do a different thing in my life and I'd like to tell you about that now. This next phase of my life has been the most extraordinary.

CHAPTER 15

✳

Looking Back

I believe it's significant to look back through my life to clarify some experiences I've had. These were times such as when I had been away from God for fifteen years. During the last year of my wandering, I had such strong desire to return to God that I thought I would lose my mind. I was so fearful of being eternally lost that I was ready to surrender. Oh people, don't ever depart from God. Don't ever depart. The little bit of fun that you have is certainly not worth the horrendous suffering that Satan will take you through. Once again people don't ever depart from God.

It was fifty-seven years ago. And oh what joy and gladness I have in this new life. I thought that was where you couldn't have any fun. That's a lie of Satan. It is the TOTAL opposite of that. I accepted the Lord as my Savior and begin an intense interest in the kingdom of God. My father was an evangelist, church planter, pastor and a prophecy teacher.

I remember as a young child and learning from the big chart he had painted which was frequently displayed across the platform of the church. Especially of interest to me were his drawings of the animals, the horns, the beautiful city and the new earth. Armed with my daddy's scrapbook, his charts and my Bible, my desire to know more about what I was reading in the Word led me to intensify my study of the Scripture. I was drawn to the supernatural of the Lord.

Being raised in a Christian home has its advantages. Having good training in my formative years has paid off for me. My family believed in living a holy life, which was enforced with discipline. Being taught the Scriptures those years most likely have played a part in my interest in God and His plan.

My favorite place to study God's Word was at my dining room table. Suddenly I could only see a thick fog and I was taken aback with it. I said Lord, *"I know there are a table, window, and chairs, but I can't see them, but it's OK."* Somehow, I knew I had entered into God's Presence even though at that time I was a new Christian and had no knowledge about His Glory. I knew it was God. I soon began to gain more knowledge through much research on the kingdom of God and Satan's domain.

After fifty-seven years, it is still my main interest as I continue to grow in God. Another time I experienced His Glory while I was working in a mill. There were people all around. I was praying silently when the Shekinah Glory appeared. I was so overcome with his Presence. I knew something was happening so I went to the rest room lounge.

The machinery was so loud that no one could hear me. I danced, worshiped and praised for quite some time. What a night! Later a group from Brownsville church was in a nearby city and I attended the service. That night the Glory Cloud appeared which was awesome! The next Sunday the cloud was in Pastor Jim's Sunday school class. I can still feel the Glory of God's Presence!

CHAPTER 16

❦

Visible Angels

I have experienced several contacts with angels, which has had a great impact on my life. For example, I clean house best when I am unhappy with something my husband Hubert had done. One day I was very upset. I was cleaning and planning to confront him when he got home from work.

Suddenly, I was completely surrounded by huge angels looking down on me with an angry frown. I decided I had better not do that today. At that point I learned how to control my thoughts and bring them under the subjection of the Spirit. Our training comes with time and experience.

Those Angels looked just like the ones I'm going to tell you about now.

Recently in church, Pastor Greg was speaking on holiness. I said to myself (not out loud), *"God would you holify me?"* And to my left side I heard someone chuckle. I thought, *"How could anyone have heard me?"* I looked around and there was a huge angel standing there with his hand over his mouth. He was actually laughing at me about the made up word I used, "holify" so I elbowed him.

I told you earlier how I had developed a communication with God. My relationship with Him is many times in the natural and I would speak to Him as though He were human and maybe be a little lighthearted with him. One example, I was sitting at the window talking to God telling Him how much I loved Him and then I thought about all the things that He had done for me that week. I said, *"God, I don't only love you, I appreciate you!"*

Immediately a small portion of the venation blinds near the top begin to slowly flow in and out softly about seven times. I looked around to see if it was my air-conditioner. It was not on. I looked to see if the wind was blowing outside but it was still. Then I realized that was a response from God. Another morning I was enjoying the sunrise and I said, *"God everything you do is more beautiful than what man has done."* Immediately I heard him say, *"Duh-a."* God speaks to me many times on my level.

I had a great dad and am using him as an example. I could sit on his lap as a child. He would read to me. I could say things to him in a joking manner. However, in public or when he got serious with me because I was doing something wrong, he was another man to me, a man of honor and integrity and one who demanded respect. Through our relationship I learned how to communicate with God. Yes! God is an awesome God. But He is also my Father and Friend.

CHAPTER 17

✤

Preparing for Eternity Future

I wish I could say that everything is wonderful when we serve the Lord here on this earth. However, it has never been that way for me. I learn obedience and grow in God when I am going through a trial of some kind. It was in March 2012 that a major setback came to my life. I was going about serving the Lord that night. I was going to help some people that didn't know how to handle a certain situation and I told God, *"If you don't help me and stay with me the enemy is going to try to harm me for this."*

It was the next morning at 3 o'clock in the morning that I suffered a stroke. I knew the enemy was trying to take me out. I told God, *"I told you if you didn't help me he would do* this situation. For the next few months I suffered two broken hips and many other setbacks but I never stopped even though I was in a wheelchair.

I continued in my prayer, studying and teaching because I always want to do the will of God and paying little attention to my own situation. At that point God begin to supply my needs according to His riches in glory by Christ Jesus. Everything I needed or wanted, it began to come in with very little effort on my part. It seems if I just desired it, it would be there soon.

2020 It has now been about eight years and I'm still in a wheelchair. I feel really bad most of the time. I continue with teaching Sunday school, a home prayer group on Tuesdays and a Bible study on Wednesdays in the complex where I live. I have spent most every day of those years in prayer study and have given myself to God. I ask Him do use me everyday doing all I can for His kingdom even though I have suffered a loss of my large muscle in my leg and I have no balance.

The only way I can walk is just a little with the walker. I am able to take care of myself but God sent me somebody for everything I need. God sent me Jeannie. What a blessing she has been. It was many years ago that a minister at our church looked toward me and said *"When God tells you to do something don't you let your body tell you what to do."* That took root in my spirit and from that day till npw I have done what God told me to do without letting my body hinder me.

Doing these years I developed a relationship with God that I never knew existed before. I discuss things with Him rather than just ask a request for Him to do something. When I ask Him a question I always receive an answer, maybe not always like I thought it would be but it comes clear and very understandable. His relationship is worth it all. If I have to be in a wheelchair for the rest of my life to experience God in ways that I have these past few years then so be it. Later I will tell you about an even deeper relationship I have developed with God and how He used me.

In March 2018, my heart began to stop and start. I was sitting in my living room when suddenly I lost consciousness with this world and entered into another dimension. I began to go backward into a tunnel with bright blue and red blocks of color. I lost consciousness to this world. Then I began to come back to this world. That was the beginning of six months of severe illness.

Debbie took me to the emergency room. Shortly after arriving there, a doctor passed by a monitor at the front desk at just the right time and saw my heart stop then start. I heard him say, *"Now I know what is happening."* They rushed me into surgery to put in a pacemaker. I was aware of what was taking place in the surgical unit. I could hear them talking about my heart going into a block and then they would shock my heart. This occurred three or four times, but I was not disturbed.

In recovery, God put a song in my heart. I began to sing *"God leads His Dear Children Along"*. Debbie was there and she began to sing along on the chorus with me. I looked up. Jesus was standing on a round white cloud singing back to us. I could not hear Him but I could tell by His gestures that He was singing. I told Debbie about it and she was amazed.

She asked what He looked like. I said, *"He looks the same as He did thirty-eight years ago when He appeared to me during a serious illness."*

I will tell you about that now. Being very ill, my daughter Laura was concerned about me. She lived in North Carolina then. She called me that afternoon and told me that I had better not die until she could come home.

Later that afternoon Jesus came and stood by my bed. He had white soft curly hair almost to the shoulders. He had a few silver hairs mangled and the beard was the same. I took special notice to the hair because I was a hairdresser at the time.

There was a mirror on the wall behind Him, but you could see the entire mirror and all of Him. He seemed to be talking to a spirit (perhaps an angel). He would look back at me and then back to the spirit. He went away and I loudly proclaimed, *"Come back! I have served you many years and I deserve to know what you're talking about!"* He came back and did the same thing again except this time He looked at me with a big smile. When I smiled back at him, it was like His smile and mine were one. This was a very strange experience. I knew that everything would be alright. He went away.

Late that evening the spirit (or angel) that was speaking with Jesus earlier came back and stood at the head of my bed. He began to show me a panoramic view of my life, how I had served the Lord many years, and this is what I have lived for. He said, *"You can choose either to go be with the Lord and receive your eternal rewards or you can choose to stay here. It is your choice."* I pondered that for awhile then I said, *"I choose to stay and declare the Word of the Lord."*

Decision came from a testimony of a minister that was in a plane crash. God gave him a choice and that's what he said. My friend Sharon brought me the tape of that testimony that afternoon and I listened to it. God plans everything so meticulously. That was a very hard choice to make at that point because there was a strong Presence of God there. I also remembered that Laura had asked me to stay here until she could come home. I was not sure about my decision, not knowing what the future held. Now I am glad I made that decision. I have had a very fruitful life and much pleasure with my family.

Back in the recovery room and having seen Jesus, my mind was not on my physical condition. We were across the hall from the nurses' station. They evidently heard us singing. My nurse was a young male. He walked over to the bed and said they were moving me to another area and he was going with me. Of course, he didn't go but I'm assuming that he heard us singing. After that, God spoke again quoting to me part of the 23rd Psalm.

He said, *"You have been through the valley of the shadow of death and have feared no evil."* I believe that is when I realized I was being tested. I assume I passed that test. At this point in my life I had surrendered everything to God to the best of my ability to serve Him and no others. I had been speaking freely with Him about this for several years.

As I was being transported to another area in the hospital, God spoke to me really clear and ask, *"Would you be willing to go THROUGH this suffering if it would help someone?"* He said He needed to test a certain person. Without knowing what suffering, or what person, I said, *"Yes."* What He seemed to be saying was that He could heal me but He needed me to do this for someone. Now I realize this is more of a spiritual matter than it is a physical matter. We all must be tested. I was aware of that.

Then I was told by the doctor that I needed surgery immediately for colon cancer. I went through the surgery. I never had any pain or discomfort and not anything that would make me think that I had eight inches of my colon removed except for weakness. I believe that came from the medication I was allergic to. It was at this time that I had an out-of-this-world experience with God.

CHAPTER 18

❋

Creation of the Universe

God takes me back to the original Creation: God began to teach me about Creation through the Scriptures. May God grant me the wisdom to explain. Hebrews11:3 NLT says, *"By faith we understand that the entire universe was formed at God's command, that what we now see did not come from anything that can be"*.

This is all taking place while I am asleep in surgery. I began to experience things out of the ordinary. I was taken out into the universe. I was standing straight. I said that because I cannot stand straight because of the stroke that I had experienced. Suddenly, I could see aempty space so huge I cannot explain it. It was dimly lit and there was nothing on either side or in front of me. I did not see Heaven. That was not the purpose of me being there. My purpose was to be tested.

However I realized that God stood beside me but I never looked toward Him. It was more like I could see and hear Him without looking. He was dressed in a soft gold robe. It was almost translucent but not transparent. He was a little taller than most men and had a shape like a man. I could see that soft golden robe but I knew if I reached out I would not be able to touch Him. I never spoke a word. However, I could understand His thoughts perfectly. He also knew my thoughts.

The first thing He said was *"In the beginning God"*, then He begin to explain God the Supreme Being. He told me He would show me His Glory and Goodness. I would never be able to explain His dynamic Power, unexplainable wisdom and abilities, the awesomeness of His Glory and the splendor of His Presence.

He said to me, *"I won't be able to allow you to remember this because you would not be able to function in the sin cursed world you live in if you remembered."* Everything good seemed to be wrapped up in One Being. He spoke to me about realms, dimensions and spheres. He told me that I could not remember that realm that I was in I do remember it did not seem unusual for me to be there.

Then He spoke again and said *"In the beginning God*

created the heavens." Then He began to show me the Creation of the universe. I have studied for many years about Heaven, Creation and God, but never did I imagine anything like this. First there was the throne of God. The Bible says there are thousands of angels around the throne. It stood out in space which was awesome.

At this time I begin to see and hear the beginning of the Creation. Stars begin to take their places, Milky Ways, Nebulous, many shapes and forms, colors and worlds. I watched as Earth took its place, prepared for mankind. Stars begin to zoom through the atmosphere. Different types of planets, moons and black holes began to take their place in the universe as God spoke to them and told them where to go.

It was as though I was questioning Him in my mind of where they came from and then God answered my thoughts saying, *"My hands hath made them."* I noticed the brilliance of the lights that were coming in from behind me but I never turned to look. I could see them without turning and He said in earthly terms, *"That is my workshop where I designed the universe and all that is in it. Every star has a name. Everything I do has a purpose and a plan and they will fulfill their duties."* Again I heard Him say, *"In the beginning God created the heavens and the earth."*

At that point He began to show me the Creation of the Earth, placing everything where it belonged. It seemed the

Garden of Eden is a very special natural and spiritual place. Everything in it is enough to sustain man forever. Every tree and plant is there to meet the needs of man. Also the animals and all of His Creation is so purposeful. I wish I had the words to explain the awesomeness of this Creation but there is no way and no words.

Connecting scriptures helps us to see more clearly. Scriptures tells us about His heavenly beings, the heavenly hosts, angels. 1st Corinthians 2:9 NKJV says, "But as it is written: "Eye has not seen, nor ear heard, Nor have entered into the heart of man The things which God has prepared for those who love Him. But God has revealed *them* to us through His Spirit." 1 Corinthians 13:12 KJV says, *"For now we see through a glass, darkly, but then face-to-face. Now I know in part; but then shall I know, even as also I am known."*

We wonder what this Creation is like. It's a beautiful green earth decorated with all kind of beautiful flowers, fruit and nut trees, blossoming trees, grass, all kind of animals, fish, birds, butterflies, skunks and snakes etc. Most Bible scholars think everything man has ever wanted to live a full and happy life was created. The Bible says that every seed bearing tree was good for food. I wonder just how many other things we have that we have not yet discovered in this world and about His provisions. It seems He brought me back to this area in what we know as Israel.

The Creation of Man: Isaiah 45:18 KJV says, *"For thus*

saith the LORD that created the heavens; God himself that formed the earth and made it; he hath established it, he created it not in vain, he formed it to be inhabited: I am the LORD; and there is none else." Someone had to keep the Garden of Eden so he created man in His image and in His likeness. He created man to have fellowship with Him, communicate with Him, someone that would worship and acknowledge Him as God.

As humans, we learn more about what we see, so looking at man you can see more of what God's natural side is like. Without the fallen nature of course but the undefiled five senses, emotion, character and all of His nature. Just because God is Spirit does not mean He does not have these characteristics.

CHAPTER 19

❋

What Are Angels

There are extraordinary activities in Heaven. Things are happening. The Seraphim have six wings, with two they cover their face, with two they cover their lower bodies, and with two they fly. They call back and forth over the Throne saying, *"Holy, Holy, Holy, is the Lord"* Isaiah 6:3 KJV.

Cherubim are said to be guardians of the Throne. They also guard the Garden of Eden and the way of the Tree of Life (Genesis). Cherubim seem to be God's main transportation as well. Ezekiel saw a storm rolling in. It turned out to be the Throne having a sea of glass in front of it. It was carried by Cherubim. Ezekiel 28:14 KJV tells us that Lucifer was a Cherub before the fall.

There is also Gabriel, a messenger of God to the Gentile nations. Michael seems to stand for Israel. There are also arch-angel and guardian angels for humans Psalms 91:11 KJV. One writer said, *"There seems to be angels watching over and taking care of everything for the Lord and us."* Some are called ministering spirits. Not all beings in Heaven are classified as angels. There seems to be other types of beings even though we may tend to classify them all as angels.

Fall of Satan: What seems to be the first reference to the morning star as an individual is in Isaiah 14:12 NIV: *"How you have fallen from heaven, O morning star, son of the dawn! You have been cast down to the earth, you who once laid low the nations!"*. The KJV and NKJV both translate "morning star" as *"Lucifer, son of the morning."* It is clear from the rest of the passage that Isaiah is referring to Satan's fall from Heaven. Satan was a created Cherub. The Bible said he was the Cherub that covered. Job 38 says, *"When the morning stars sang together, and all the sons of God shouted for joy?"* Angels are innumerable.

God originally created everything to be good. However Satan and man polluted the whole world and our atmosphere. That is why Jesus came to earth, to restore us and the earth.

His New Heaven and New Earth is possibly going to be like He originally created it. In order for it to be that way, there has to be a restoration and cleansing from all the evil Satan and man has caused. This must be done by fire, not water like in the days of Noah. Water washes but fire destroys. He has already preformed a restoration on the people. 2 Corinthians 5:17 KJV says, *"Therefore, if any man is in Christ, he is a new creature: old things are passed away; behold, all things are become new."*

The person did not pass away, only the evil that was in him. Scripture says that about the earth using the same Greek word. Old things will pass away and all things become new, not to be remembered any more. It's the same as our sins.

In Genesis, God told Adam to till the garden. He put him to work soon after the Creation. Work is a great part of God's plan. Hebrews 2:11 KJV explains how He is no longer ashamed to call us brothers and sisters. Therefore our work is to God and has undying value, whether it is provinces or nations working alongside God. As one writer puts it, *"We are co-creators with him."* That would be on a lower level.

Jesus said we are joint heirs with Him and will reign with Him. There is an outstanding purpose for what we do here on earth. The book of Hebrews explains how not only we, but the earth is in need of a restoration. Jesus is the One supremely in charge of the Creation and only by working in Him are we restored to fellowship with God. This alone makes us capable to take our place again as vice-regents of God on earth. Humanity's created destiny is being achieved in Christ in whom we find the pattern. Evil plays a strong hand at present and Heaven and earth is in need of radical restoration. Hebrews is trying to show this because it is now subject to evil. Therefore it is subject to radical restoration.

Malachi 4:

Sickness from medication: After God stopped talking and showing me things, I was back in intensive care. Next, the medication I was allergic to begin to make me weak so that i could not eat or drink for many days. My team of doctors came in that did the pacemaker surgery. I knew something had to be done or I wasn't going to make it. I became very serious with my doctor and told him something had to be done, that I was getting worse when they had promised i would be all better after the pacemaker surgery.

But in the meantime, just after the doctor left the room, Laura, Debbie and my granddaughter Heather came in the room. I told them to get the bottle of oil out of the drawer and anoint me and pray THE prayer of faith. This was like a command from Heaven as the medication was devastating to me. After anointing me with oil we started praying and then Debbie stopped and said, *"I don't know how to pray!"*

Then she thought about what the Bible says, *"When you don't know what to pray let the spirit pray through you because he knows what to pray."* So we all stopped and begin to pray in the spirit, all four of us. It was at that point that I began to get thirsty and hungry that was so different from what it had been. I had not been able to eat or drink very much for over two weeks, just one or two bites at a time. It was from that point I started to improve from the effects of the medication. For those of you who are not Pentecostal, praying in the spirit is when you pray in a language that you have not learned, tongues of men and of angels.

A Covenant with God: Before I explain what happened next, I want to remind you of what I told you earlier in the book, about an agreement that I made with God in about 1963. I told Him, *"If you will help me I will do everything I can for you throughout all my life because I don't want to be an ordinary Christian and I don't want to receive an ordinary reward. I want the most extraordinary place in Heaven that I can possibly have."* Since then I have thoroughly enjoyed my walk with the Lord. I still want to do everything I can as long as I can for God. I Believe I will receive my reward but I would do it for Him at this point in my walk with God. If there were no rewards I have kept my agreement through the years, no matter how hard the suffering, pain or distress. I never stopped and I have tried not to slow down. I intend to pick up momentum the rest of the way home. In the next story, there was an attack of Satan during this time. He was going to try to convince me that I have given up. But the Bible says he is a liar and the truth is not in him.

CHAPTER 20

❦

Satanic Attack

Looking back at the question about God asking me to suffer so someone could be tried He said again, *"I really need you to do this for me."* It seemed this next test I'm going through at this point is the purpose of all my suffering. I was incoherent much of the time. That is when God or Satan would speak. Each time the enemy would come and put negative thoughts in my mind, before long, God would come and teach me truth and something positive. This was the first attack from Satan.

I was no longer on the earth. I wonder if this is one of the times my heart had stopped. I could see myself as though I was suspended somewhere in space. There was a bank of white clouds behind me and I was not standing straight. I was bent over. I could see a spirit and at the time I believe it to be God. I should have known better at the time because of my surroundings.

The spirit said, *"You are wondering where you are. You are actually on the outskirts of my dwelling place."* I believe he was trying to imitate God, taking me into the universe. I could see him. Everything was black and dark but he resembled an orange ball with an orange glow around it. He is a poor imitator. A week or two later, I begin to examine that scene. And now I know for sure that it was the enemy.

Second horrendous attack: As I pondered this encounter, I believe God let me stand with Him and see the universe being created so I could make a choice. We have to make choices all through our lives.

I believe God had given Satan permission to do what he is doing to me now. Being with God I realize that He is more natural than we think and more spiritual than we think just like He had told me before. I thank God He counted me worthy to go through this experience. I'm thinking that God let me stand with Him and see the universe being created so I would have a choice of whom I would believe.

As I was waking up from the colon surgery, I had an unordinary attack from Satan. He spoke out of the most hideous blackness of darkness saying, *"You say you believe in God and Heaven. How do you know it's true as many people believe many different things but that does not make it true. Neither does your faith make God true. Look up, what do you see?"*

There is no universe, I could not see a thing it was all black, no stars or anything. I thought, *"Even if I can't see it, I still believe it is there."* It seems I am now outside but it was still all black and darkness. He kept saying that many people believe many things about Heaven and God but it does not make it true, it's just a figment of your imagination. My mind was clouded with his accusations yet, there was not a single doubt in my mind. I continued in that darkness for a long time until I was very weary and he began to tell me *"You have lost the reward you asked God for years ago, because you told God you did not want to suffer."*

Of course I don't remember doing that. He told me that i did that while I was asleep. If that is true how do I remember all the other thing she and God that happened while I was asleep? He continued bombarding my mind with negative thoughts for days. He was very convincing. I am really tired of this fierce battle. I began to strongly rebuke him. Then I declared, *"I'm going with Jesus all the way. I choose to believe in Heaven and in Jesus even if I can't see it now."*

And I spoke to God saying, *"God, I do not believe I did that. I cannot believe that I would give up anything in Heaven to avoid a little suffering down here. I never did it before and I don't believe I've done it now."* For weeks Satan attacked my mind telling me I did give it up but I couldn't remember. He was extremely convincing. He kept saying that I would not have anything except Heaven. Sometimes it would be days between these encounters with God and with the enemy. Then God would challenge me to see the truth and reminding me of miracles He had done for me.

Back in the hospital: Things in the hospital room are changing. I am still sleeping most of the time. I awoke and my dad who has been dead for about 44 years appeared at the head of my bed dressed as he did in the 1030's and 1940's. He appeared as he had been working in the field. He didn't say anything, he just walked around.

Then I saw my sister and two brothers. They were much younger than they were when they went to be with the Lord. They were standing still side by side and not talking. They were just on the other side of the wooden rail fence which we had around our property in those days. Behind them was a huge field but there was not a blade of grass and not a tree. It was totally empty. Everything was dead. My dad was also behind the fence up toward my head.

My girls heard me say, *"How did you get here?"* My girls asked, *"Who do you see?"* I said. *"Papa, can't you see him?"* Most everyone thought for sure, at that point, I was not going to make it. But I knew better. That lasted for quite a while and then they were gone. I begin to try to tell people about it but the Lord did not seem to approve of me telling it, so I didn't mention it but to just two or three people. Later Satan said, *"Did you see the dead grass? Did you see the old fence that represents that you have nothing laid up in Heaven? It's all gone and is dead."*

Knowing God was with me, I had explicit confidence in that He would not allow Satan to defeat me. I didn't have a dread or fear as my heart was fixed. I began to realize something did not seem right and I pondered what was going on. I began to realize it was Satan sending familiar spirits. You might ask, *"What is a familiar spirit?"* They are evil spirits, wicked spirits that follow you around on earth familiarizing themselves with your mannerisms and dress etc so they can imitate you later.

Then I realized that was the way people dressed in the 1930's and 1940's so it was those spirits from that time which had been observing my family. They had come in the form of my family and that was not a visitation from my family from God. I believe Satan did that to make my family think I was not going to live. I am delighted to say, the spirits didn't do a good job at all. My sister never wore red and she had a red blouse on. I suppose the spirits didn't know all that much about them as we were always a lively family.

God preformed many miracles for me. One miracle was

shortly after Debbie and Wes, my daughter and son-in-law were married. They both took a job at a convenience store. It was a nighttime job. I always thought that was not safe. One night around 11 pm after I went to bed, God spoke to me that one of them was in danger. I thought it was Debbie. I got up, dressed and drove to the store. She assured me that everything was alright so I got into my car and headed home. I became even more disturbed so I held my hand out toward the store and said, *"Regardless of Debbie or Wesley, regardless of the devil or anything else, nobody will enter that store to do harm and Debbie and Wesley will not work there anymore."*

I went home but the next morning Debbie called and said, *"Mama, the store where Wesley works was robbed last night and one man was killed another wounded."* The man killed was standing where Wesley would have normally been. She wondered why I didn't pray for both stores. I did pray for Wesley's safety but not for the store. I was thinking God was warning me about her store.

I am now thinking that I need to be more thoughtful about how I pray. We are here on this earth to be armed and available when He needs someone. This is what God was speaking of when he asked me would if I go through this. I do know for sure now that it was me that He was testing and you will understand it better as you go along in the book and why I had experiences with both God and Satan.

Along the way I have surrendered everything to God to the best of my ability and to serve Him and people. I have been speaking freely with Him about this for several years. I am thinking He's testing me concerning that. I was not fully conscious of what was going on. Then I heard Laura singing *"Soon and very soon we are going to see the King"*.

At that point I don't think she had much hope of me recovering. It seemed that was what everyone was thinking. However, God took care of everything concerning the surgery. I didn't seem to be affected except for the weakness and I have been improving since. No, I'm still not completely well, but I am on my way.

CHAPTER 21

❧

What Is God Actually Like?

How can we know God? Before the sickness I had asked God this question. In my private place of worship, I have spent years alone with God. During my confinement I have developed a very close relationship with God I asked Him, *"What are you really like?"* He replied, *"I am more natural than you think and I am more spiritual than you think."* I understood from that encounter that I needed to upgrade my knowledge of Him.

I found man has more of the nature of God than I thought, but He also was more of a spiritual being than I realized. I began an intensive study about God and His

Creation. We know His spiritual attributes are all-powerful, all-knowing and all-present.

But do we really understand what that means? We understand His natural side better. Man was made in the image of God. Looking at man's emotions and characteristics helps us to know His nature better. Man has God's nature, but at man's best, he seems to give too much control to self and the enemy.

CHAPTER 22

❦

The Creation of Heaven and the Earth

God made man, IN HIS IMAGE. I asked God many years ago why He created such a great universe and earth. He spoke back to my heart that it was for His Son and His Son's Bride. Isaiah 45:18 KJV says, *"For thus saith the LORD that created the heavens; God himself that formed the earth and made it; he hath established it, he created it not in vain, he formed it to be inhabited: I am the LORD; and there is none else."* **Colossians 1:16-20 KJV says,** *"For by him were all things created, that are in heaven, and that are in earth, visible and invisible, whether they be thrones, or dominions, or principalities, or powers: all things were created by him, and for him."*

There were many of my friends and family that came and helped during this time of illness. I was thinking what I could do for them. God spoke to me and said, *"The ones that have done anything for you will receive a whopping reward."* I thought that "extraordinary" sounded better but God spoke back to my heart and said, *"I did not say extraordinary, I said whopping."* I looked the words up and whopping has a stronger meaning than extraordinary. God always knows best.

Concerning my time to go home, it was back in the early1990's that I asked God, *"When will I be going home?"* His immediate answer was, *"Your life is like a sermon. You are in the third and last point. You just don't know how long that point is."* I settled for that at the time. Then, I wanted to know just how long that would take. It was about 2006 that I asked Him the same question and again, He answered immediately and said, *"You can't come home until you get your work done."*

Recently I have asked him that question again and the answer was the same. I keep asking him this question because many times and especially recently I really didn't think I would make it through the night or that day. I asked Him that again last week. His answer was different this time. He said, *"Work is almost done but you will have to clean up some litter that has been scattered around the court yard, by you and some others and then you need to make your part of the world look good before you leave."*

I wondered what needed cleaning. He showed me something that I had been saying to people that was leaving the wrong impression. I will go ahead and write it down so if any of you have heard me say this, you will understand it. I have said that I heard a minister speak once about not allowing your body to tell you what to do.

And that is what I wanted to say except I suppose I did not make it clear. It's the thing that God tells you to do. If He tells you to do it, He will give you the strength to do it. You don't let your body tell you what to do in that case. There are a few other people I need to straighten this out with and that will clean up part of the clutter.

Then He talked to me about Job saying, *"Most people think that was a unique experience."* But it seemed to be an example to everyone because we all must be tried. For this reason we should suffer without complaining, knowing that others who have gone on before us have suffered. Hebrews 12:1 KJV says since we are surrounded by such a great cloud of witnesses.

Through the years God has sent His ministers with His Words to declare what will happen in the last days and showing things that are taking place in Heaven now. God has spent many thousands of years trying to develop a people that would follow, love and worship Him so he could give them the things that He has prepared. He has always provided them for us and one of the things He has provided are angels. As we look at them we can see these angels have abilities. He tells us that we have ministering spirits that are sent to minister to the Saints.

Synopsis of the Different types of Angels: Some of these angels God sends down to watch over His people and to help us in times of need.

1. Seraphim's, Worshipers Isaiah 6:1 KJV
2. Cherubim's, cover Gods throne Genesis 3:24 Ezekiel 1:6 KJV
3. Archangels, Michael and Gabriel, special messengers Daniel 10:13 Michael Has spiritual authority. (He is the Chief Prince). He seems to stand for Israel. Gabriel stands more for the Church. He came to Mary and Hezekiah.
4. Principalities, rulers heads of some angels Ephesians 1:21 KJV God's angels.
5. Powers, Warrior and Thrones, Ezekiel 1:21-28 KJV Thrones carry God's Throne.
6. Dominions Ephesians 1:21 KJV Gods Angels
7. Ministering spirits, Hebrews 1:14 KJV Minister to heirs of salvation.
8. Guardian angels

There seems to be an angel for every purpose under Heaven. The next category lists the ones we have to be wary of. Now, I know how to combat them. We are much more powerful than they are because we have Christ Jesus in our hearts.

Ephesians 6:12 KJV fallen angels

Principalities chief ruler of the unseen world system

First in rank or first in existence gives out unholy orders to other evil spirits. He is the antichrist spirit.

Powers they try to overpower you physically and mentally in every way.

Powers of darkness blind people to the truth.

Spiritual wickedness that is evil in both the spiritual and physical realm.

Our hope is in Christ Jesus, Romans 8:38 KJV says, *"For I am persuaded that neither death nor life, nor angels nor principalities nor powers, nor things present nor things to come, can separate me from the love of God."*

Another challenge: Seeing we are facing and will face evil forces, we must always be alert. For those of you who are suffering from spiritual or emotional struggles, financial or any other, we must brace ourselves to combat the spirit world.

Don't Give Up Don't Give Out Don't Give In

A. DONT GIVE UP: During these times of trouble be careful not to surrender to Satan's suggestions such as...

There's no need to try, your family will never change. You are not expected to be hurt by your companion. You just need to get out of that marriage.

If you have been crushed by: feebleness, sin, troubles *Isaiah* 43:24 KJV

A bruised reed shall He not break.

He will not carry on the work of destruction and entirely crush or break it. And the idea is, that He will not make those already broken down with a sense of sin and with calamity, more wretched. He will have an affectionate regard for the brokenhearted, the humble, the penitent and the afflicted.

Isaiah 61:1 KJV says of the Messiah, *"He hath sent me to bind up the broken-hearted"* and to the declaration in Isaiah 50:4 KJV, said that I should know how to speak a word in season to him that is weary. God said He will carry you through. Take it to Jesus and don't forget to leave it there.

B. DON'T GIVE OUT: Isaiah 43:24 KJV says that smoking flax shall he not quench (wick on a lamp) till he sends forth judgment unto victory.

Satan will tell you that you have toiled so long, you've given out and Its not worth the struggle, you are tired, take a break, think about how long you have been doing this, and there is no need to keep preying. We must be aware of those things and refuse to listen.

C. DON'T GIVE IN: Satan will try to say, why struggle with sin? If you will do this one more time, that will satisfy you. It won't hurt anything, God forgives. Then you can get back on the straight and narrow. Remember that Sampson laid his head in Delilahs lap just one time too many.

Don't ever give up, don't ever give out, and don't ever give in.

CHAPTER 23

❧

The Rapture

The next event on this earth seems to be the Rapture of the Church. I Thessalonians 4:15-17 KJV says, *"In a moment, in the twinkling of an eye, at the last trump: the Trumpet shall sound, and the dead in Christ shall rise."* Then a marvelous thing will happen. We're all going to the marriage supper of the Lamb. Can you imagine the state of the art decorations, food and fellowship? It's the beginning of His promise of our joy forevermore. It tops all banquets.

Jesus told His disciples at the last supper or communion, He would not drink of the cup anymore until He drank it new in the kingdom. Taking communion seals our relationship with Him. God uses things we know about to explain His plan.

A good example is a wedding. It starts like this. The bridegroom comes to the bride's house where he asks her father for his daughter's hand in marriage. He brings a dowry. Before he leaves they take communion to seal their relationship. After that, if a couple separates, there has to be a divorce. Then the groom goes to prepare a home for them. The father tells his son when to go get his bride. Likewise, Jesus said, *I go to prepare a place for you."* The Father will tell Jesus when everything is ready and to come for us (our communion has a much deeper meaning than what we understand).

Another example is when Abraham sent his servant to get a bride for his son Isaac. Father God sent His Holy Spirit to get His Son Jesus, a bride. *"We will understand it better by and by".* After this event, we will all return to the earth with Jesus for Him to set up His Millennium Kingdom.

Battle of Armageddon: It appears that the world is spinning faster and faster, heading toward the end of the age and the sure coming rule of Christ (Philippians10). Revelation 16:14 ESV says, "For *they are demonic spirits, performing signs, who go abroad to the kings of the whole world, to assemble them for battle on the great day of God the* Almighty."

Just before Christ returns to this earth the battle of Armageddon is raging. Then hundred pound hailstones falls, Isaiah 13:9 KJV, Matthew 24:27 KJV. After that, He takes care of the evil army that is trying to destroy God's people. You don't want to mess with Gods family.

Then Jesus begins to set up His kingdom here on earth. He will rule and we will reign with Him for 1,000 years. When He returns we don't go to Heaven at that time, not for a thousand years. You can't have peace as long as the devil is around. God goes ahead and takes care of that in verse 20 that says, *"Then I saw an angel descending from heaven, holding in his hand the key to the abyss and a huge chain. He seized the dragon the ancient serpent, who is the devil and Satan and tied him up for a thousand years. The angel then threw him into the abyss and locked and sealed it so that he could not deceive the nations until the one thousand years were finished."*

The 1,000 year reign of Christ is peace, prosperity and long life. How awesome this world will be. Revelation 20:7-9 ESV says, *"And when the thousand years are ended Satan will be released from his prison and will come out to deceive the nations that are at the four corners of the earth, Gog and Magog, to gather them for battle; their number is like the sand of the sea. And they marched up over the broad plain of the earth and surrounded the camp of the saints and the beloved city, but fire came down from heaven and consumed them. And the devil who deceived them was thrown into the lake of fire and sulfur, where the beast and the false prophet are too, and they will be tormented there day and night forever and ever."*

Great White Throne Judgment: As things are winding down, we have one more judgment and that is for the wicked at the great white throne judgment. Do everything you can to avoid this judgment. *"Then I saw a large white throne and the one who was seated on it; the earth and the heaven fled from his presence, and no place was found for them. And I saw the dead, the great and the small, standing before the throne. Then books were opened, and another book was opened, the book of life. So the dead were judged by what was written in the books, according to their deeds. The sea gave up the dead that were in it, and Death and Hades gave up the dead that were in them, and each one was judged according to his deeds. Then Death and Hades were thrown into the lake of fire. This is the second death, the lake of fire."*

If anyone's name was not found written in the book of life, that person was thrown into the lake of fire. Then it gets even more awesome, a day we all longed for. This world, all evil and lies and hypocrisy, will be totally consumed with fire. The atmosphere where Satan set up his kingdom will totally roll back like a scroll. The elements will melt with fervent heat. No more room for him in the air.

It is the evil works of man, the enemy and his kingdom that will be burned up, the area where Satan has set up his copycat throne and ruled over the principalities of the air. It sounds like God gets rid of everything that is not holy and that is His plan. He is replacing it with brand-new things beyond our comprehension and they are for our pleasure.

CHAPTER 24

❧

The New Jerusalem

God is now ready to show us our Capitol City. In Revelation 21:2 GNT John says, *"I saw the Holy city, the New Jerusalem coming out of Heaven from God."* What an experience! A foursquare, gold city studded with all kinds of gems at the foundation. Its brilliance is incomprehensible. Inside the city, he describes God's throne as a sea of glass before it.

Nations will walk in the light of that city and kings will bring their riches into it. I heard it described like this:

The City at the center of the future Heaven is called the New Jerusalem. Everyone knows what a city is. It's a place with buildings, streets and residences occupied by people and subject to a common government. Cities have inhabitants, visitors, bustling activity, cultural events, and gatherings involving music, the arts, education, religion, entertainment and athletics. If the capital city of the New Earth doesn't have these defining characteristics of a city, it would seem misleading for Scripture to repeatedly call it a city.

Over the years, people have told me they can't get excited about the New Jerusalem because they don't like cities. But this city will be different. It will have all the advantages we associate with earthly cities but none of the disadvantages. The city will be filled with natural wonders, magnificent architecture, thriving culture, but it will have no crime, pollution, sirens, traffic fatalities, garbage, or homelessness. It will truly be Heaven on Earth.

The Good News Translation of Revelation 21:24 says, *"The gates of that city have names written thereon. These names are the names of the Twelve Tribes of the Sons of Israel."* This means that New Jerusalem is the future permanent home of the redeemed of the nation of Israel. Since the twelve gates have the names of the twelve tribes of the sons of Israel written on them, and since there are twelve foundation stones with the names of the twelve apostles on them, New Jerusalem is to be the home of both the redeemed of Israel and of the Church.

There is a correlation, I believe, between the 24 names and the fact that in Heaven there are 24 elders (Revelation 4:4,10; 5:8,11:16;19:4 KJV). I believe the 24 elders include twelve elders of Israel and twelve elders of the Church. They are presently in Heaven, but they will inhabit New Jerusalem throughout eternity. It is impossible to state with certainty the identities of any of these elders. It is altogether possible that the twelve elders representing the Church are the twelve apostles.

What is the significance of the fact that each gate is a pearl? John Phillips writes, *"How appropriate! All other precious gems are metals or stones, but a pearl is a gem formed within the oyster, the only one formed by living flesh. The humble oyster receives an irritation or a wound, and around the offending article that has penetrated and hurt it, the oyster builds a pearl. The pearl, we might say, is the answer of the oyster to that which injured it. The glory land is God's answer, in Christ, to wicked men who crucified Heaven's beloved and put Him to open shame. How like God it is to make the gates of the New Jerusalem of pearl."*

"As they come and go, the saints will be forever reminded, as they pass the gates of glory, that access to God's home is only because of Calvary. Think of the size of those gates! Think of the supernatural pearls from which they are made! What gigantic suffering is symbolized by those gates of pearl! Throughout the endless ages we shall be reminded by those

pearly gates of the immensity of the sufferings of Christ. Those pearls, hung eternally at the access routes to glory, will remind us forever of One who hung upon a tree and whose answer to those who injured Him was to invite them to share His home." as quoted in *The MacArthur New Testament Commentary*, Revelation 12-21.

The New Heaven and New Earth: Paul, John and Isaiah describe what happens next. Israel possesses their land. Jesus has taken care of this world's system and replacing it with His. Look at what Paul says in 1 Corinthians 15:24 JUB, "Then *comes* the end, when he shall have delivered up the kingdom to God, even the Father, when he shall have put down all rule and all authority and power." In Revelation 11:15 TLV John said, *"The seventh angel blew his trumpet and there were loud voices in heaven saying the kingdom of this world has become the kingdom of our God and of Jesus Christ. And He will reign forever and ever."*

Isaiah 60:21 NASB says it this way, *"Then all your people will be righteous; they will possess the land forever; they are the branch of my planting, the work of my hands, so that I may be glorified."* Isaiah 9:7 says, *"The increase of his government and peace there shall be no and, upon the throne of David, and upon his kingdom, to order it, and to establish it with judgment and with justice from henceforth even for ever the Lord of hosts will perform it."*

The Lord said to Abram after Lot had parted from him, *"Look* around from where *you* are, *All* the *land* that *you see I will* give to *you* and your offspring forever"* The Lord will bring about for Abraham what He has promised him.

CHAPTER 25

✳

O Glorious Day

This is the day that all Christians have been longing for. The sufferings that are going on now will be no more, no more pain, no more death, no more sorrow, crying, or heartaches. They will all be gone forever. John saw a New Heaven and New Earth. Why a new? Will it be like this earth? Because this earth has been polluted by Satan, its pollution has to go.

Ephesians 3:21 KJV says, *"Unto him be glory in the church by Christ Jesus throughout all ages, world without end. Amen."* Do you ever wonder what we will be doing? Will we have to work? Many people believe that whatever your heart desires is possible. He knows our every thought and knows what we enjoy doing. He made us and He will meet your every desire. We will live in our new home happily ever after.

When He said, *"I make all things new"*, that could mean it will be made new, as we were made new in Christ. The word "new" is the same Greek word used when He said He would make all things new on the New Earth, "koinos". At least we know it will be wonderful with the absence of evil and that will be awesome.

It seems that we are being prepared now on this earth for what we will be doing in Heaven. If you're using the gifts that God has given you here, work will be a pleasure then. Where there is a kingdom there is lots of work and activities. The best description of our resurrected bodies is Jesus. He said He was the first fruits of all resurrection. Look at His resurrected body. He ate, cooked, you could touch him, He walked around and talked. It appears that we are going to be very active in our new life and new environment.

God created the Heavens and the earth, then He told Adam to keep the Garden of Eden. I wonder if this New Earth will be more like restoration than a new one. Doesn't sound like we will just be floating around on some cloud idle all day. It sounds more like we will be enjoying our duties praising and worshiping God forever.

There will be, according to the Bible, an earth, nations, kingdoms and kings. Jesus said, *"Eyes have not seen, nor ears heard, neither has it entered into the hearts of man what God has prepared for those who love Him. But it has been revealed to those who love Him,"* Revelations 11:15. This helps us to understand what the Word means when it says in Romans 8:18, *"I reckon that the sufferings of this present time are not worthy to be compared with the glory that awaits us."*

I challenge for you today is, if you don't know Jesus I would like to help you get to know Him. Then find a wonderful church that teaches the entire Word of God and that will lead you into a deeper walk with God. If you want to be a part of this kingdom without end, then you have an open invitation to come to Jesus and start your journey to that Holy City, New Jerusalem.

Call or text me at 334-430-8555 or write me at 285 Sylvest Dr., Montgomery, AL 36117. I will be happy to introduce you to our wonderful Lord and further instruct you on how to live.